HAUNTED SAPULPA

HAUNTED SAPULPA

TANYA McCOY AND STACEY PRICE

Haunted America

Published by Haunted America
A division of The History Press
An imprint of Arcadia Publishing
Charleston, SC
www.historypress.com

First published 2025

Manufactured in the United States

ISBN 9781467159647

Library of Congress Control Number: 2025941217

Notice: The information in this book is true and complete to the best of our knowledge. It is offered without guarantee on the part of the authors or The History Press. The authors and The History Press disclaim all liability in connection with the use of this book.

DEDICATION

I (Stacey) would like to dedicate this book to my parents, who allowed me to watch horror movies at the age of ten, and my husband, who provides unwavering support for my overseas and stateside trips in search of all things spooky and who works extra hard to make sure I always have the coolest new equipment available. Love ya, babe!

CONTENTS

1
THE HISTORY OF SAPULPA

Sapulpa, located about twelve miles southwest of Tulsa on historic Route 66, is in Creek County and serves as the county seat. Around 1850, a full-blooded Lower Creek Native American, James Sapulpa, came to Indian Territory and established a trading post. In 1886, with the arrival of the railroad, a depot was built. James became friends with many of the railroad workers, and it was decided to name the station after him. It would become known as Sapulpa Station. Not long after this, a post office was built. The town became incorporated on March 31, 1898. A few years before incorporation, the Euchee Mission Boarding School was built to educate Native American children—or so was the claim. These boarding schools were established to force a new way of life and beliefs on the children, who were often forcefully removed from their homes and families to prevent them from retaining or learning their tribes' cultures. For the first few decades, the population of Sapulpa rapidly grew, and with the discovery of oil and other natural resources in and around the area, the town began to flourish. As with most towns, Sapulpa's population fluctuated, depending on the economy. But like in any other town, with prosperity came crime, and it appears that Sapulpa saw its fair share of crime over the years. Historic downtown Sapulpa offers many things to see and do. It has a small-town feel as you walk the streets, with several little shops and eateries to enjoy. Each year, the town hosts a Christmas Shute, where all the stores that line the downtown area, as well as a few

Above: Old Sapulpa Depot. *Sapulpa Historical Museum.*

Left: The post office on Hobson Avenue. *Sapulpa Historical Society.*

Opposite: James Sapulpa, known as Chief Sapulpa. *Sapulpa Historical Museum.*

pop-up buildings, decorate lavishly to create a unique and memorable Christmastime event for all ages. In 2025, the city postponed its event due to street repairs, but you can be sure that this event will kick off once again in 2026, bigger and better than ever before!

Times have changed in the town of Sapulpa. Many businesses have come and gone, many still struggle to carry on, and although some businesses no longer exist, one thing is sure: the spirits of those who one thrived there still linger. James Sapulpa, along with a few of his family members, rest peacefully in a small family plot located in the middle of a quiet neighborhood, marked by only a few lonely headstones and single plaque that depicts the final resting place of their earthly remains. Throughout the rest of the town, you

will find a few more cemeteries that also house the earthly remains of some of Sapulpa's most notable residents and founding fathers. Each cemetery holds its own version of spooky tales and folklore, should one ever wish to hear. But the appearances of ghosts aren't the only bits of paranormal activity that Sapulpa is known for. Bigfoot, unexplained UFOs and even skinwalkers have been witnessed throughout the years. With such a vast array of paranormal activity surrounding the area, Sapulpa is the perfect location for anyone wishing to have a paranormal experience of their own. Just remember to be careful of what you wish for—you may end up witnessing more than you ever truly wished to see!

2
THE ROOTS OF ROUTE 66

World War I had just ended, and the nation was entering a new era of growth and expansion. With the growth of the mass production of automobiles and the need for so many to escape the heartache of their loved ones lost to war, families began to migrate west, toward the newer states, including the previous Indian Territory, now known as Oklahoma. It was during the war that it became abruptly clear that a more efficient highway system was sorely needed, not only for the benefit of the individual traveler but also for the advancement of the military's war effort to preserve and protect the infrastructure of the United States. The Good Roads Movement was originally started in the late 1800s, and a local participant by the name of Cyrus Avery would soon become a major advocate for the development and arrival of historic Route 66 in Oklahoma.

Cyrus Avery first arrived at Oklahoma as a young boy traveling with his family in a covered wagon. They left their home in Pennsylvania behind to start a new life in the far west, then known as Indian Territory. Once here, he continued to make his living farming and then branching out into the oil industry and taking on various civil duties. One such duty was serving as the chairman of the state's highway commission. It was during this time that he earned himself a designation that would be forever attached to his legacy. He became known as the "father of Route 66." Avery was instrumental in the formation of Route 66 through Oklahoma, ensuring the famous route would find its way through his adopted home state. He was involved in the founding of the U.S. Highway Route 66 Association, which helped

A resident with a car. *Gasoline Alley Classics.*

boost tourism along the route and played a major role in ensuring the entire highway was paved from Chicago to California. One such campaign used to raise awareness of the newest route took place in 1928 and was known as the "Bunion Derby." The Bunion Derby was a footrace that spanned over 2,400 miles along the length of the new Route 66 and then went on to New York to complete the journey. The event was organized by a sports agent known as C.C. "Cash and Carry" Pyle. It was a grueling eighty-four-day footrace across country that left participants exposed to various types of weather events and conditions. The sum of $25,000 was offered as the grand prize, equal to almost $500,000 today; 199 men started the race, but only 55 ever crossed the finish line. It was one of Oklahoma's own who went on to claim the prize. Andy Payne, a young Cherokee man of only twenty years, received the money and title, landing him a place in history along with the famous route. The campaign proved to be a success, and by the late 1930s, Route 66 was completely paved from start to finish and soon became known as the "Main Street of America."

3

PARANORMAL 101

Whenever I (Tanya McCoy) teach a class, conduct a TED talk or give a simple interview for an event, TV or a newspaper, one question is always asked: "What is a ghost?" It is a complex question, yet it has one simple answer: it is energy. Now, if you ask me what a haunting is, the answer wouldn't be so simple. You see, there are various types of hauntings, each deserving of their own explanation. Take a photographic haunting for example. It is not really a haunting at all; rather, it is a movie being played over and over in time. The CDs and DVDs that are used to record movies and music contain a crystal element that helps preserve the image or sound onto the device. Many locations can do the same since the Earth is basically one huge crystal. So, when someone has a traumatic experience, whether happy or sad, those emotions can be recorded in time and attached to that location. That does not mean a person is haunting that location; rather, a memory is. However, if, one day, that spirit happens to turn to you to acknowledge your presence, that spirit has now become what we call an intelligent haunting. That means the spirit of someone—or even something—abides there and is capable of interacting with you. Today, when most people think of a haunting, they picture a poltergeist-type haunting, much like the one featured in the major motion picture of the same name. But unlike the motion picture, the likelihood of your backyard being filled with the caskets from an old graveyard is highly unlikely. That's not to say that there isn't such a thing as a poltergeist haunting. The word *poltergeist* simply means "noisy ghost." But there are times when poltergeist-like activity is not really the result of a ghost at all. Now, do not get me wrong, you might experience seeing what appears to be the living dead walking through your kitchen, looking forlorn and ghastly white, but do not worry, it is most likely just your teenager going through a very emotional time in life. Unfortunately for them—and us—their sad and negative energy can often cause electrical disturbances, causing lights to flicker off and on, garage doors to open and close on their own or objects to move. My oldest daughter's telepathic energy was so strong during her teenage years that she could shut my wi-fi system down with a single burst of melodramatic depression or anxiety.

When most people do experience true poltergeist activity, they often believe that the spirit is negative and out to do them harm. This is not always the case. Some ghosts are simply creating activity to get your attention. This activity can take place when an intelligent spirit has learned how to manipulate energy enough to move objects with their own energy. However, if a knife suddenly comes flying toward your head, rest assured, that spirit has ill intent.

The last and most traumatic type of haunting is a demonic haunting. People are often quick to call a haunting demonic, but just because you have a mean spirit, that does not mean it's demonic. Demonic hauntings are actually few and far between. There has been a sudden rise in appearances over the past decade, but this is possibly due to the increased curiosity in the occult and summoning. Depending on your religion or faith—or even your choice to not believe—there are a set number or demons and angels in the hierarchy, and new ones are not created, since they are believed to have never been human. So, for most, your odds of actually encountering a demonic spirit are slim, unless, of course, you are involved in this field of paranormal research. If you decide that you wish to actively conduct research in this field, I suggest doing your research first. It is not for the faint of heart, and while seeing might be believing, once you have seen something, it cannot be unseen. And as always, be respectful. The spirits you will run into were once just like you. Please treat them with the respect and empathy that everyone deserves.

4
Major Disasters

Every state is subject to disasters, and Oklahoma has seen its fair share of them. Often, paranormal activity can be linked to a location based on the contents of the ground there. Perhaps the location has a high density of limestone or major underground water systems and high levels of minerals conducting electrical currents. Other times, it can simply be due to the major disasters and loss of life the area has seen. Oklahoma is part of the most active area in the country for tornados. Being in the center of Tornado Alley, the state has suffered billions of dollars in damage this past decade alone thanks to its unstable weather patterns, but it has also been featured in numerous television shows and Hollywood movies. The most recent film featuring the destruction of tornados that was shot here in Oklahoma was the 2024 film *Twisters*, directed by Lee Isaac Chung. This movie was considered a "part two" to the original 1996 movie *Twister*, directed by Jan de Bont. In the 2024 version, the lead actress, Kiernan Shipka, actually states that she grew up on a farm in Sapulpa, Oklahoma, linking the city to Hollywood once again. However, this particular movie also lays claim to this author's heart since I (Tanya) was actually able to join in the hundreds who gained background parts in the film, along with my husband. This was not the first major film featuring tornadoes in Oklahoma that I got to work on, but it was amazing to be able to join in on the fun. While filming a movie about tornados can be fun and exhilarating, actually being caught up in one is a different story. For many citizens of Sapulpa, they learned all too quickly just how deadly Oklahoma weather can be.

Holy heck, it's a twister!

In the early morning hours of May 4, 1960, a cold front began to sweep into Oklahoma. The weather services called for severe thunderstorms, fierce winds and damaging hail. That evening, a small twister touched down on the southeast part of town, damaging several homes in Sapulpa and uprooting a few trees. Thankfully, only one person sustained minor injuries that night. Unfortunately, the worst was far from over. On May 5, a second tornado touched down, and this time, the town was not so lucky. The tornado touched down on the northwest part of town and caused a substantial amount of damage. The twister traveled north, up the historic Route 66, destroying hundreds of homes in its wake and claiming the lives of three people. The city declared a state of emergency following the tornado's destruction. On the morning of May 6, the city faced another deadly tornado, as reports claimed, "An ugly, death-bearing tornado leaped from the skies....The cold, gray light of dawn Friday signaled the start of a search through the mass of rubble and mud for five persons unaccounted for. As late as 1:00 p.m. Friday, reports were received that a fourth fatality had been recorded here, but this is not confirmed officially." The city lost power and the ability to pump water, which caused even more issues for the citizens of Sapulpa. Another major loss for the city was the

Yale Theater fire. *Sapulpa Historical Society.*

destruction of the Booker T. Washington High School and the Mt. Olive Baptist Church.

Tornados are not the only disasters the town of Sapulpa has had to endure over the past century. The city bore witness to multiple fires that claimed businesses, property and lives. One of the most notable fires was the Hotel Loraine fire of 1949. The hotel was a three-story building, not including the ground floor, located on the corner of Main and Lee Streets. The hotel contained seventy guest rooms, but there were only thirty-five guests registered in the hotel that night. The fire was suspected to have started in the kitchen area around 1:00 a.m. and quickly spread to the floors above. Guests began yelling out that the hotel was on fire to help wake the other guest in the hotel. Many were finding it difficult to escape the rising flames, so they began to toss mattresses out the windows to the

Opposite: Loraine Hotel. *Sapulpa Historical Society.*

This page, top: Sapulpa Fire Department. *Sapulpa Historical Society.*

This page, bottom: First National Bank, Main Street. *Sapulpa Historical Museum.*

sidewalk below. People began leaping from the burning building with hope of escaping the flames that were rising higher and higher into the darkened sky. Firefighters began to arrive, and efforts were made to extinguish the flames. They fought on throughout the night, but the Loraine would not recover from the devastation. Two men were reported missing in the wake of the fire. Louis Vincent, the first reported missing, was found deceased in the rubble, still wrapped in his blanket. Jack Graves remained listed as missing. From 1899 through the present day, the Main Street district of Sapulpa has suffered multiple fires throughout the years; they destroyed the buildings, but the citizens rebuilt. The lives of the victims and fire personnel that were lost mark a dark time in Sapulpa's history, but their memories live on in our minds and hearts, and we'll never forget their sacrifice and dedication to the City of Sapulpa.

5

COPS, ROBBERS, MURDER AND MAYHEM

Like most towns, Sapulpa has a long history of events steeped in mystery and murder. In December 1922, Sapulpa faced its own possible race riot due to the mastermind planning of one small group. On December 31, 1922, local police received an anonymous call about a possible shooting near a local café owned by Ed Glass (also the owner of the Black funeral home known as Glass Funeral Home). When the police arrived, they were unable to locate the trouble, so they approached the Glass Café. On opening the door, Officers Floyd Sellers and J.T. Hildreth, as well as a few of the other officers who responded, began to come under fire as a spray of bullets were hurled toward them from the darkened room. The first officers to fall were Patrolman S.E. Brumley and his partner R.D. Adams. Officers Sellers, Hildreth and J.F. Loveland fought their way into the restaurant, each one sustaining an injury. Sellers, while returning fire on the assailants, injured one culprit as they fled out the back door toward their escape vehicle. A local newspaper article read, "Chief of Police Ralph Morey stated he felt sure the situation was well in hand and no race riot or disturbance was feared. Three [citizens] had been arrested as suspected of complications in the shooting; five others had been taken into custody for questioning." However, it was believed that Chief Morey was the initial target. There had been several incidents within a few days; anonymous calls were placed, asking for police assistance, and with each call, the caller requested Chief Morey be present.

Chief Morey, hoping to prevent a repeat of what Tulsa had witnessed just one year before, added more patrols to help keep order in the town of Sapulpa, and he even encouraged all the citizens from the community, no matter their race, to keep the peace. It was stated, "A delegation of six [Black residents] from Colored Businessmen's Association appeared to the City Commissioners to ask that a [Black] Policeman to be put in the addition. Their spokesman said that the fact that no [Black] officer was employed, was causing resentment and might lead to serious trouble. He said that the delegation represented the law-abiding element who wished to prevent any trouble."

The following response was given by a city official in response to the accusations that many newspapers of the time had been making toward the Sapulpa incident being similar to the Tulsa Race Massacre.

> *Keep Cool. Now is the time for cool, deliberate judgment. Sapulpa is sitting on a powder keg, lighting matches. The city is stirred perhaps as never before. One or two hotheads can easily produce a race riot. Sapulpa does not want the stigma attached to her name that Tulsa has. No use to condemn the entire* [Black] *race for what a half dozen irresponsible* [culprits] *have done. Let's be calm, quiet, deliberate and above all let's preserve the fair name of our city.... There is no need for more bloodshed. There is no need for further killings unless someone drops the match into the powder keg. Surly, no one in Sapulpa wants that responsibility....Let's protect and preserve the fair name of the best city in the southwest....*
>
> *Cool heads at a time when members of two races are engaged in bloodshed, that more than often than not results in uncalled for damages, killings, and injuries, are something to be highly valued. They can give* [a] *community a reputation for careful, timely action that points toward a commendable enforcement of the law. Lack of them, replaced by the panicky element, can stamp the blackest of marks across the community's name.... The result is that a crisis has probably been passed, and Sapulpa will not add a costly, uncherished chapter of race rioting to her history. A handful of* [people] *are blamed for last night's trouble.... These are the ones to be captured and punished.... Cool heads can do Sapulpa a big service now. Let's see that congratulations stay in order.*

Many members of the town reached out to the officers and city commissioners to aid in their efforts.

> *Plenty of tasty, hot coffee and a bite to eat may be found at the grocery store of S.L. James* [a Black businessman] *in the business district of the addition. James, his wife, and other* [Black] *citizens have kept an open house every night since the shooting affray and all guards are welcome for hot coffee and choice variety of food to make the long nights seem shorter.... City and County Department heads were profuse in their admiration of the manner in which Sapulpa citizens conducted themselves, both by keeping down any racial trouble and through their services as members of the patrol squads in the addition.*

It was through the quick actions and level-headed thinking of the officials of Sapulpa that the citizens were able to avoid a potential race riot during one of the most heated times in American's history. It should also be noted at this time that the city did in fact have a Black officer the year prior to this event. Richard E. Nelson was Sapulpa's first Black policeman. He was praised for his work with the sheriff's department. He received his first injury on the job when responding to a domestic disturbance; he was nearly shot in the face by the aggressor. It was the same type of wound that would claim his life ten years later. Nelson was gunned down along with his passengers David Croston and Floyd Conner during a traffic accident with Legus Brown. Nelson and Croston were fatally shot in the head. Brown turned himself in, proclaiming he had shot them in self-defense. He was acquitted a year later.

There would be other famous shootouts noted along Sapulpa's historical timeline. The year was 1934, the Great Depression was in full swing and crime was at an all-time high. A jewelry store in Sand Springs, just ten miles north of Sapulpa, had just been robbed. The Sapulpa Police Department received a call regarding some suspicious-looking men hanging around town. Officer Gage, along with a few other men, drove around town searching for the men, but they were unable to find them. Later, they received another call with an anonymous tip stating that the men were staying at a small farmhouse just a quarter of a mile from the old Highway 66, northeast of the city. Gage returned to the police station to gather more assistance. Chief Tom Brumley, along with Special Officer Floyd Sellers, joined Deputy Sheriff Gage to gather guns and ammunition. Sheriff Willis Strange arrived at that time, and all four men gathered into his car and headed toward the farmhouse.

The farmhouse belonged to a local farmer named Lee Davis. With the rear of the house overlooking the Sapulpa/Tulsa highway, it offered anyone inside a clear view of any approaching cars. When the officers first arrived

Lawmen of Sapulpa. *Sapulpa Historical Society.*

on the scene, they noticed a man peering out the window, but he quickly dodged back out of sight. When the officers exited their car, Gage headed to the corner of the house. There, he recognized two men, Aussie Elliott and Eldon Wilson. They were the two men who had recently escaped the Pawhuska Jail, where they had been awaiting a fifty-year sentence. Officer Gage yelled out, demanding they stop. Instead, the two men ran back into the house. Chief Brumley yelled out, "Whoever is in there, come out now!" Davis, the owner of the house, emerged. Brumley ordered him to get the others outside, too. Davis replied, "Sure, sure." Then he headed back into the house. Strange continued to demand that the men show themselves. The two outlaws, Elliott and Wilson, walked toward the door, but what the officers didn't know was that there was a third outlaw hiding in the cellar at the back of the house. Dubert Carolin, alias Raymond Moore, stood up and began firing at the police. Chief Brumley was hit in the chest and quickly went down. Then Elliott and Wilson joined in on the gunfight, opening fire on the lawmen. When the gunfight was over, Elliot was found dead. Wilson had sustained a bullet wound to the abdomen and was found lying on the porch, holding his stomach. The third outlaw, Carolin, began running as Sellers and Gage took pursuit. The three exchanged gunfire, but Carolin was able to reach a set of trees nearby and escape into the woods.

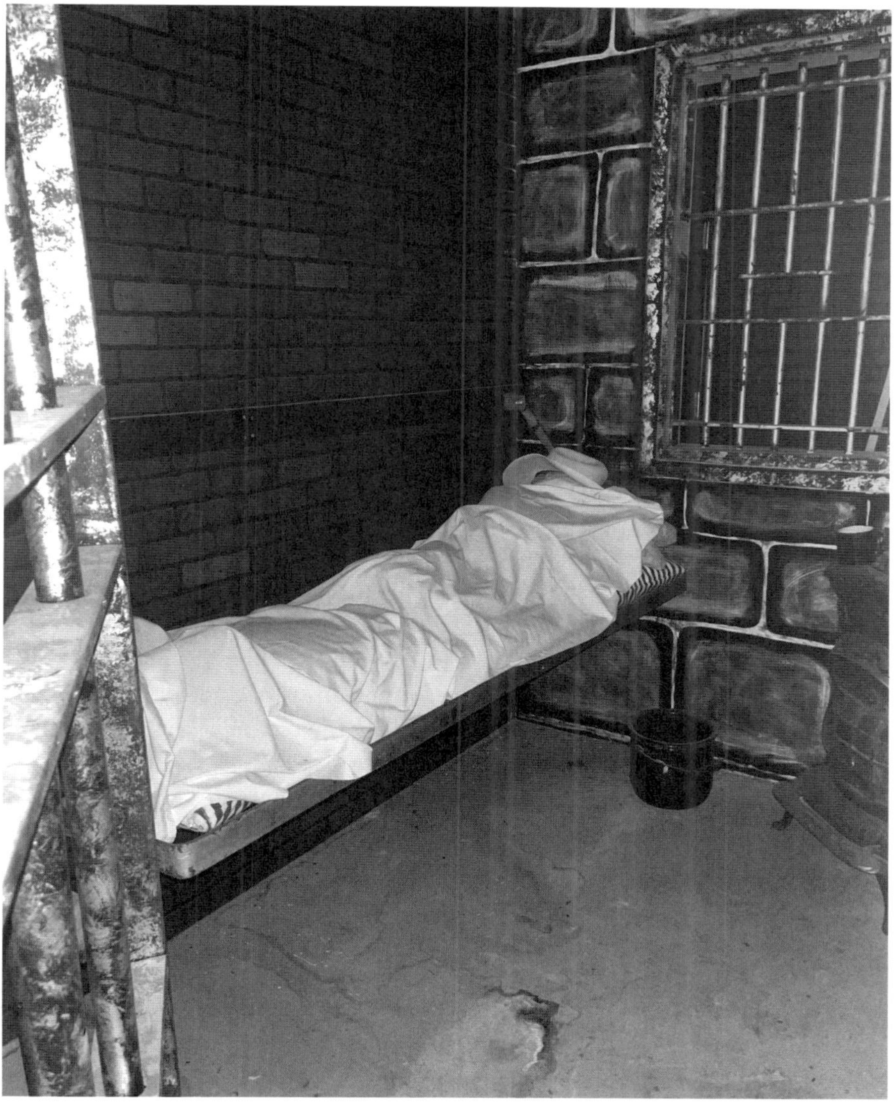

Re-created jail cell. *Tanya McCoy.*

Officer Gage ran to a nearby neighbor's house to call in the event. An ambulance arrived, along with three more officers and two firemen. Sheriff Strange escorted the body of Chief Brumley back into town. Lee Davis was booked into jail along with Eldon Wilson, and the Tulsa police were called in to assist in the manhunt of outlaw Carolin. Wilson bled to death on his jail cell floor sixteen hours later from the stomach wound he received during the shootout.

Officer C.P. Lloyd, along with two other officers, set out in search of Carolin. A nearby neighbor by the name of Gambrill, after hearing the shootout take place, spotted Carolin hiding behind a woodpile and hurried down the road to inform the police. By the time the police arrived, he had already left. The number of police officers on the hunt began to grow. They continued to search the area and soon discovered a long ditch. Believing the outlaw was hiding there, eight officers began closing in. As Officer Lloyd approached the ditch, he spotted Carolin and quickly drew his gun. Unfortunately, Carolin did the same. Both men fired. Shots rang out. As the smoke settled, it was clear Officer Lloyd had fallen—Carolin claimed yet another officer's life. The remaining seven officers opened fire, pummeling Carolin's body with bullets. In the end, it was the consensus of the seven remaining officers that it was Lloyd's shot that had killed Carolin.

After learning of this story, my (Tanya's) team set out to try to contact the spirit of Eldon Wilson while investigating the Creek County Courthouse, which currently holds the town's jail. The team was unable to gain any response from a spirit claiming to be the infamous outlaw Wilson. However, through further research I was able to obtain information that leads me to believe the jail he passed away in was actually the old jail located behind the old city hall building.

The building that was once home to city hall is now home to a small boutique called the Frilly Flamingos. The old jail is located directly behind the four-story building. When I arrived at the site, I was greeted by the owner of the business and allowed into the area that once served as a jail. The bars of the cells have long been removed; however, the names of previous inmates remain carved into the historic bricks inside the building. We are hoping to investigate the site in the near future to see if the spirit of the outlaw remains today. I've also been told that the larger building has an old plaque dating to the years of the Cold War that lists the building as a fallout shelter. Luckily, it's a location that has not had to be utilized this way—and hopefully it never will.

Another tragic story took place the same year as the shootout. During the Great Depression, many people suffered from various mental illnesses due to the strain of the times. This next story centers on another tragic tale of a father who decided he simply couldn't take it anymore.

Living on the outskirts of town in a little, shabby, rundown house was the Barrett family. Chester Barrett and his wife and eight children lived a meager life like most did at the time, barely scraping by, just trying to make ends meet. Providing food and shelter for one's family had become a daily struggle for most people, and the Barrett family were no exception. For a few, they paid the ultimate price: their lives. These were the reasons given by a father who said he was pressed beyond his limits and led to inflict unjust pain and injury on his family.

Chester Barrett was quoted as saying, "I couldn't bear it any longer," as he began to tell the sordid details of events that took place in May 1934. Barrett stated he had been ill for several months, leaving him unable to work. "I hadn't any money, and my family was starving," he said. "I couldn't bear it any longer." Barrett decided to kill his family. Three of his younger daughters, ranging in age from two to six, lost their lives to poisons fed to them by someone they loved and trusted. His wife and four remaining children, ranging in age from five to twelve, became severely ill but survived. The eighth child, a seven-month-old baby girl, was not served the poison. Barrett claimed that he couldn't bring himself to harm the baby and hoped that someone would adopt her instead.

Barrett admitted to a previous attempt to poison his family on April 30 that same year, but he said he lost his nerve. On May 5, he attempted it again, and this time, he succeeded. Since the family had just recovered from a recent attack of the measles, he told them he was giving them quinine mixed in milk to ward off fevers. He was able to purchase the poison by saying he was going to use it to kill rats. He then administered a dose to himself. But in a state of panic or remorse, Barrett staggered over to a nearby neighbor's house and stated that he and his family were suffering from an illness or food poisoning. The county physician was called, but it was too late to save the three young girls. It was later discovered that Barrett also kept a mistress and had fathered a child with her, but he elected to not poison them.

An investigation was launched. Soon after, Barrett confessed to his dastardly deeds that led to the death and injury of his family. Chester Barrett was tried and found guilty that same year. On September 20, 1935, Barrett met his own fate, as he was escorted to be executed by the electric chair for his actions against his family and the murder of three innocent girls. His execution brought this tragic story to an end.

Not all outlaws who visited the town of Sapulpa lived there. One of the most notorious of these outlaws lived only a few miles away in the city of Tulsa. She was a bootlegger named Cleo Mae Epps. Also known as the "queen of the bootleggers," Epps ran with the Dixie Mafia. The Dixie Mafia was based out of Biloxi, Mississippi, and dealt in illegal drugs, alcohol and stolen goods. Many members belonged to a traveling gang who would break into businesses and private residential homes; they would also murder for hire, participate in bribery and money laundering and influence peddling. While the Epps gang was operating in the Tulsa area, Sapulpa saw some of this similar crime taking place, which leads me to believe she may have been operating the Sapulpa area as well.

Cleo Mae Epps was an educated woman. She graduated from high school at the age of sixteen and began teaching two years later. Her first marriage was to a lawyer from Tulsa whom she later divorced due to his incessant drinking. In 1936, she married Cecil Epps, who became a bootlegger. Despite Cleo being strictly against whiskey, Cecil's alcoholism left him incapable of conducting business. With the bills piling high, Cleo was forced to take over the business. Cecil and Cleo divorced in the 1950s, but by that time, Cleo had already earned herself the title of the bootlegging queen. In 1959, Prohibition was reversed in Oklahoma, but Epps's troubles were far from over. In 1966, Epps was accused of running a multimillion-dollar moonshine operation. However, the verdict was quickly overturned, but with her continued contact with the Dixie Mafia, Epps remained under the watchful eye of the law. In 1970, Judge Nelson was up for re-election against a new candidate by the name of Charles Pope. Nelson was predicted to win the election, but the Dixie Mafia had other plans. They decided they wanted to remove Nelson from the race entirely. Career criminals Lester Pugh and Albert McDonald, friends of Charles Pope, visited their old friend Cleo Epps. There, they removed five sticks of dynamite from her farm. Growing suspicious of their intent, she informed Creek County Investigator Jack McKenzie. On August 25, Judge Nelson's car exploded in his driveway with him in it. Nelson survived but was critically injured. Epps agreed to testify, but only if she could do so in disguise. Word leaked about her testimony, alerting the two men to her involvement in the case. On November 12, Epps met up with McDonald to conduct some business for an illegal bootlegging shipment. Her yellow pickup was found later, abandoned with only her purse inside. In February 1971, an anonymous tip led investigators to an old septic tank on an abandoned farm, where her body was discovered. Epps's head had been wrapped in a towel, secured with a rubber band. A single bullet hole to the back of her head had ended the life of the queen of the bootleggers. Pugh and McDonald were both sentenced and later died in jail, ending their reign of terror in the Tulsa area.

In January 1976, another vicious murder took place in the small town of Sapulpa, one that would rock the community and leave a lasting mark on the history of the town. The sordid tale took place at the local high school, where two of the school's coaches went missing one day. Since both of the men taught classes during the day, their disappearances should have been noticed early that morning. However, the alarm was not raised until the police from the nearby town of Bixby, Oklahoma, located a stack of blood-soaked papers belonging to one of men scattered around a local highway.

Football season was over. Coach Jerry Bailey had just resigned as the head coach of the Sapulpa team and was actively looking for a new coaching position. On January 22, 1976, Bailey was seen leaving the high school parking lot with assistant coach Paul Reagor in Reagor's car. When neither Bailey nor Reagor returned to teach their first class, inquiries were made. Bailey's wife, also a teacher at Sapulpa High School, learned that her husband had not been in class. She tried to call home to see if he had gone home for some reason. There was no one there to take her call. A few hours later, she was called to the office, where she met with local law enforcement who asked if she knew her husband's whereabouts. She was informed that personal papers belonging to her husband had been found scattered along a road near Bixby and appeared to be covered in blood.

Law enforcement from Sapulpa, Bixby and Tulsa joined together in the hunt for the two missing men. Neither were found that day. As night came, the hunt was called off but began again in the morning. With the use of a police helicopter and a news crew, Reagor's car was discovered hidden in some overgrown weeds near an old, abandoned farmhouse on Mingo Road. When police examined the car, they noticed its bumper had blood on it. When they opened the trunk, they found the body of Coach Jerry Bailey. He had been stabbed twenty-two times. They searched around the vehicle, looking for any signs of Couch Reagor, but they were unable to locate him near the car. They eventually discovered him inside the abandoned farmhouse, lying on an old mattress, his shirt stained with blood. The blood, however, was not his own; rather, it was the blood of his close friend Jerry Bailey, blood he had been covered in when he chose to take the life of his friend and colleague. His motive was anger. Once Bailey had resigned his position, it was believed by many that Reagor would be hired to replace him as head coach. Reagor also believed this. When the school decided to hire someone else, Reagor felt betrayed by his friend. That feeling soon turned to rage, and that rage led to murder. Reagor was convicted of second-degree murder and was sentenced to ten years to life in prison. But he never spent a day behind bars. Four years later, while out on bond and awaiting his appeal, Reagor died from natural causes. Despite having lost his wife and family over his murderous deeds, Reagor never truly paid for his actions, and Bailey's family, as well as the community, was left forever torn by the evil actions of one man. The memory of Coach Bailey remains within the walls of the Sapulpa High School and in the community. His life was taken so many years ago, but his spirit will forever live on in the memories of this community.

6

CREEK COUNTY COURTHOUSE

Located at 222 East Dewey Avenue is an architectural masterpiece known as the Creek County Courthouse. Constructed in 1914 in the Greek Revival/Neoclassical architectural style, this three-story building, constructed with granite blocks, continues to serve as the county courthouse over a century later.

Throughout the years, this courthouse has seen its fair share of crimes, murders and deaths. Including the sentencing of outlaw Lee Davis, found guilty of the murder of Police Chief T.J. Brumley and his Deputy C.P. Lloyd, this building has witnessed many tragedies throughout the years. As this building has such an intriguing history, it is no wonder our team was excited to jump at the chance to investigate it.

The courthouse has some unique and interesting features, such as a doorknob next to the first-floor bailiff stand. The fourth floor used to house the old jail, and there, you can still see the original bars above one of the doors. The building has four floors, including a basement. With such a vast space to investigate, we were left with the difficult decision of where to start the night's investigation.

We began our night by conducting an EMF detector sweep throughout the building to rule out areas where our equipment might expect interference and to familiarize ourselves with any hazards we might not detect in the dark. Once our initial sweep was complete, we headed up to the fourth floor. Knowing that the fourth floor used to contain the old jail, we assumed that the probability of experiencing paranormal activity might be good.

However, it was on the first floor where our team encountered much more paranormal activity.

Our first location was one of the courtrooms on the first floor. It was in this location where our first EVP sessions were conducted. The following are our findings from our first session.

FIRST-FLOOR EVP SESSION

Amanda: *Is there someone here who wants to communicate? Have a little chit chat?*
[Flashlight turns on.]
Yes [flashes twice].
Amanda: *Are you excited that they're here?*
Yes [flashlight on].
Amanda: *Do you like the fact that we are here?*
Stacey: *Would you rather us not be here?*
[The cat ball lights up.]

Opposite: Creek County Courthouse. *Sapulpa Historical Society.*

Above: Old City Jail. *Tanya McCoy.*

Amanda: *We aren't here to be pushy or nosey.*

[Flashlight turns on.]

Amanda: *Is that what you think? Are you trying to get us to leave?*

Stacey: *If you're sick of us and want us to get out of here, turn on another device.*

Amanda: *Turn both of them on if you want us to leave.*

[The flashlights both turn on at this point.]

Amanda: *If you want us to leave, can you light up the cat ball again?*

[The flashlight keeps going, but the cat ball does not light up.]

Teresa: *They're not going to do anything now; they already told us to go.*

Stacey: *Is this your courtroom? Do you want us to leave your courtroom?*

[The motion sensor music box goes off when no one is moving at that time.]

[We then began hearing footsteps, and the music box went off again.]

Amanda: *Is that you* [we] *hear walking around? I heard you make that music box go off again.*

[Flashlight turns on.]

Stacey: *It just drained my battery on my phone, and my handheld video camera both went off at the same time after being charged all day.*

Teresa: *OK we'll leave now.*

[End of session.]

We headed up to the second-floor courtroom and took the tripwire (which lights up whenever it's touched or tripped); the music box set to sound when motion is detected; the spirit candle, which, in theory, lights up when a surge of energy is present; and a mini-mag flashlight that is set to be turned off and on by spirit manipulation. The following is the transcript of the session.

Second-Floor EVP Session

[The flashlight turns on twice.]

Stacey: *If there's someone that wants to communicate, please touch the candle on the podium.*

[The candle doesn't turn on; however, the flashlight turns on instead.]

Stacey: *Can you please light up one of our devices, please?*
[The flashlight turns on.]
Stacey: *Are you male?*
[The flashlight doesn't react.]
Stacey: *If you're a female, will you light up the flashlight, please?*
[The flashlight gives no response.]
Stacey: *If you want us to stay here, you're going to have to light up more lights so we know you want to communicate with us. Are you familiar with one of the faces in the room right now? You should know him; he works here* [referring to our escort deputy]. *You can touch the candle or the flashlight.*
[The flashlight gives no response.]
Stacey: *If you want us to leave, you're going to have to light up a light. If you do, we will take it as a sign that you want us to leave.*
[The flashlight turns on.]
Teresa: *Do you want to talk to us? If so, will you turn on the flashlight?*
Teresa: *Stacey asked if you wanted us to leave. Do you want us to leave?*
Stacey: *I need you to be clear that you want us to leave; we will respect that.*
[The flashlight turns on again, so we decided to call it quits in that room.]

We continued to another courtroom where highly emotional cases have been tried over the years. The following is a transcript from that courtroom.

Courtroom No. 3 EVP Session

Stacey: *Is there anyone here that wants to communicate with us?*
[The flashlight blinks on two times indicating a yes.]
Stacey: *If there's a male presence in here, can you shine a flashlight again?*
[No response from the flashlight.]
Stacey: *Can you say the name of someone in this room right now?*

We asked, at this point, if the spirit was a victim of a crime. After receiving no response, we then asked if the spirit was one of the lawyers, judges or court reporters who used to reside there. Still, we received no response. It wasn't until we asked if the spirit we were communicating with was perhaps a previous bailiff that received our response. A strong K2 (EMP) level was recorded in answer to our question, indicating a possible identification of the ghostly presence. It was during this time that Amanda noticed a dark shadow lurking in the jury box and causing our motion sensor music box to alert us to the activity there.

(EVP session continues)

Amanda: *Was that someone else over here in the chairs with me that I saw? Whoever was over here with me, can you let me see you again?*

[Amanda, at this time, hears a series of taps, taps that were also caught on one of our audio devices.] [Amanda, at this time, invites the ghost to come to touch her hand, which the K2 responds to with a large red spike.]

Amanda: *Can you come back over here, please? Come sit by me. I see you lighting up my machine.*

[The flashlight turns on again.]

Amanda: *Were you a member of a jury here in a case?*

[The flashlight has no response.]

Amanda: *Were you someone who was on trial here in this room?*

[The flashlight turns on.]

[We reposition the motion sensor to a certain area and begin questioning again.]

Amanda: *Can you please light up that green light next to me if you're still here?*

[The flashlight turns on once again.]

Amanda: *There's a red light on the floor now if you walk in front of it. It will play that pretty song. Can you do that for us?*

[Amanda states that she is starting to feel chills on her right arm, which is on the same side as the K2 meter and motion detector. Teresa also detects a change in temperature in the jury box.]

Amanda: *Do you know where Teresa's K2 meter is?*

[The flashlight turns on and goes off twice.]

Amanda: *Can you come to touch my hand? It's OK with me. I have a bracelet that I wear on my wrist if you want to play with the beads on my bracelet.*

[The flashlight turns on.]

Rachel: *Is it getting colder here?*

Amanda: *Are there spirits here that are making it colder?*

[The flashlight gives no response.]

Amanda: *Is there somebody on trial here?*

[The EMF detector spikes to a full red, indicating a possible presence. Suddenly, we all hear the sounds of disembodied footsteps and the sound of pants rubbing together, as if someone is walking by, but no one in the courtroom is moving.]

[During this session, Susan, another team member, had been monitoring the EVP session on the equipment. Susan was able to correspond the findings with the EVPs in correlation with the questions and equipment alarms, as well as Amanda hearing a disembodied exhale at the same time.]

Susan: *Who was talking to me earlier and saying, "My baby, my baby?" If you are still here, can you turn on one of these devices?*

[The flashlight turns on.]

Susan: *Was your baby hurt?*

[The flashlight turns on again.]

Susan: *Is your baby your child?*

[No response from the flashlight.]

Susan: *Is your baby your spouse or girlfriend?*

[The flashlight immediately turns on.]

Susan: *Were you here because your girlfriend or spouse was hurt?*

[The flashlight turns on for yes again.]

Susan: *Were you charged with your baby's injuries? Did they think you were the one who did it?*

[The flashlight turns on again.]

Susan: *Are you charged with hurting her, is that why you are so frustrated?*

[The flashlight gives no response.]

Susan: *Are you innocent of her injuries?*

[The flashlight immediately turns on.]

Susan: *Do you want to tell me your name?*

[The flashlight gives no response.]

Susan: *If you are innocent—*

[The flashlight immediately turns on again.]

Susan: *We got that—yes—we know you're saying that you are innocent. Was the person that harmed your baby ever caught?*

[The flashlight turns on two times, indicating a *yes* response.]

Susan: *Were you acquitted?*

[The flashlight gives no response.]

Susan: *Were you wrongly convicted?*

[The flashlight gives no response.]

Rachel: *Were charges against you dropped?*

[The flashlight gives no response.]

Teresa: *Were you found innocent by the jury or the judge?*

[The flashlight gives no response.]

Rachel: *Are you still here?*

[The flashlight turns on.]

Susan: *Is your baby your spouse or your girlfriend?*

[The spirit candle turns on this time for yes.]

Susan: *Is the candle someone else? If it's someone else, can you turn it off please? If whoever lit that up is the same person we've been talking to, can you turn the candle off, please?*

[The flashlight turns on.]

[Stacey reminds the group that the last time she was in this room, on SLS, she saw two figures as stickmen on the camera.]

Stacey: *So, is there a male and a female in here? I think there's a male and a female. Can you light up the flashlight or candle, please? Are there two males?*

[The flashlight blinks two times.]

Stacey: *Are there two males talking to us this evening? Can you turn the flashlight or candle back on?*

[This time, neither the flashlight nor the candle responds.]

Stacey: *Was there a male and female a while ago? We have had two people communicating with us.*

[Neither the flashlight nor the candle responds.]

Susan: *Is the male I was talking to earlier still here?*

[The flashlight turns on.]

[During this time, we recorded loud bangs and thumps on our recording device, but these sounds were not heard or noted by anyone in the room.]

Susan: *Do you want me to keep on asking questions about what happened to your baby?*

[The flashlight does not turn on.]

Stacey: *Is it too painful to talk about it? Were you able to reunite with your baby?*

[The flashlight turns on, indicating yes again.]

[On the recorder, we heard many knocks and a large bang in the hallway during this time.]

Stacey: *Is there another spirit in the hallway trying to communicate with us? Can you set off one of those lights?*

[The flashlight gives no response.]

Susan: *Whoever lit up the candle, are you male? If you* [are,] *would* [you] *please touch it again? I want to talk to the person who lit up the candle earlier. Go ahead and turn off the flashlight, please.*

[Another loud bang was recorded on the audio recorder, but it was not noted by the group.]

Susan: *Clearly, you have a message for us. Is the person that lit up the candle earlier still here?*

[The flashlight turns on again.]

[Teresa notes that the temperature has dropped significantly, low enough to give her chills.]

Susan: *Is there something that you need to tell us? If so, light up the lights.*

[The flashlight comes on.]

Susan: *Are you just wanting to talk to us because you're happy that someone knows you're here?*

[The flashlight immediately blinks on and then turns on two more times.]

Susan: *My gentleman with the baby, do you still want to talk to us about that case?*

[The candle is turned on.]

Stacey: *If that was a no—that you don't want to talk to us about that anymore—can you light up the flashlight?*

[The flashlight turned on, so we ended the session.]

[End of EVP session.]

After going through all the courtrooms and reading through various lines of questioning using equipment like flashlights, cat balls that light up, spirit candles, a music box, a K2 meter and an SLS camera for detection and communication, we decided to head to the basement for the final communication of the night.

As we went down the stairs to the basement of the courtroom, we immediately felt the EMF levels increase due to the overhead electrical wiring. The levels are so high that it makes your hair stand on end. In the basement area, I (Stacey) noticed two areas where piles of dirt could be seen opening up into a crawl space under the floor. Had I had the proper clothing, I might have found myself venturing into the dark, musky corners in search of treasure untold beneath the granite cornerstones of the old courthouse. Instead, it was down to business as we started our next session in the basement of the old courthouse. With equipment set up and members in place, we began our next session.

Basement Estes

Susan: *Lots of activity tonight—seems like you really want to talk to us.*

Amanda: *Let me know when you want me to go under* [referring to an Estes session].

Susan: *Go ahead now. We are in the basement and we have already got a lot of flashlight activity, and the candle is on now. How many spirits are with us tonight?*

[Flashlight turns on.]

Susan: *How many spirits do we have with this tonight? Amanda, can you hear what we are saying?* [As a reminder to the reader, when an Estes session is performed, the one responding is wearing noise-canceling headphones hooked into a spirit box and cannot hear the questions being asked. They only respond with words or sentences they hear from the spirit box.]

Amanda: *Here, I'm with you* [Amanda repeating words from the spirit box].

Susan: *Colin, are you by yourself, or do you have other spirits with you?*

[Flashlight turns on again. The spirit candle also lights up at this time.]

Susan: *Do you live down here in the basement all the time?*

Amanda: *Word.*

Susan: *Did you die in this basement?*

[Flashlight turns on.]

Susan: *Did you work in this basement when you were alive? Did you live on this land before there was a basement here?*
Amanda: *Next.*
Susan: *Are you male?*
[Flashlight turns on.]
Susan: *Are you female?*
[Flashlight turns on again. The candle is still on at this point.]
Susan: *Are you an adult?*
Amanda: *Fear. I see.*
Susan: *Are you a child? You don't have to be afraid of us. We just want to talk to you.*
Amanda: *Get out.*
Susan: *Why should we get out?*
Amanda: *Say your vows.*
Susan: *What kind of vows?*
[Flashlight turns on again.]
Amanda: *Are you?*
Susan: *Am I what? Are you human? Because I am.*
[Flashlight is still on.]
Susan: *You have nothing to fear from us. We just want to talk to you.*
Amanda: *Once.*
Susan: *You were once human? What are you now?*
Amanda: *Help him.*
Susan: *Who are you helping? We will help if we can. Who do you want us to help?*
[At this point, Susan said she received full-body chills.]
Amanda: *Think.*
Susan: *Is it someone who worked in this building?*
Amanda: *We gotta get out.*
Susan: *Why do we have to get out?*
Amanda: *I am unforgettable.*
Susan: *Well, I will agree with that so far. Are you able to leave this building? Do you have a name? What is your name, please?*
[The spirit candle turns itself back on.]
Susan: *Did you build this building? Were you involved in the construction of this building?*
Amanda: *You're joking.*
Susan: *I don't mean to be joking, I am trying to ask serious questions.*
Amanda: *Talk.*

Susan: *OK, were you involved in the construction of this building?*
[Flashlight turns on.]
Susan: *What is the period?*
[Amanda relates to us that she just heard a scream.]
Amanda: *That's important.*
Susan: *That she's gonna scream? Why?*
[Flashlight turns on again.]
Amanda: *Really? Once.*
[It is about this time that the boiler makes a sound that sounds like a scream, and we all jump a little bit and laugh afterward.]
Susan: *Are you saying that there is a correlation between building it?*
[Flashlight turns on again.]
Rachel: *Are you trying to tell us yes with the flashlight?*
[The spirit candle turns on.]
Stacey: *Please talk through Amanda and use the radio.*
Susan: *Is there a message that you need to tell us? Do we need to get a message to someone for you?*
[Flashlight turns on again.]
Amanda: *Hold the candle.*
[Flashlight turns on.]
Amanda: *Don't.*
Susan: *OK, I won't. Where is the House of Horrors?*
[Amanda relates to us that everything on the spirit box has gone weirdly quiet.]
Susan: *But the lights are still going on. Are you still going to talk through Amanda?*
[The spirit candle turns on.]
Amanda: *The house was fine.*
Susan: *OK, so it's been a while since you've been at the house, but it was fine.*
Amanda: *How are you doing?*
Susan: *I'm doing fine. How are you doing?*
[Amanda relates to us that she heard another scream.]
Susan: *Wow, are you in pain?*
Amanda: *No.*
Susan: *Are you in emotional pain? I'm going to try again. Would you please tell me your name? I know you said you built it* [this building] *earlier but that didn't seem like—*
Amanda: *I'm not done.*

Susan: *Tell us whatever you'd like to tell us. We are here to listen to you.*
Amanda: *Oh my God.*
Susan: *What is that about? Why did you say that?*
[Flashlight turns on again.]
Susan: *Are you OK? If you are OK, please talk through Amanda.*
Amanda: *There is blood.*
Susan: *Whose blood?*
Amanda: *Rage. Stop it.*
Susan: *Is someone hurting you? Is that what happened to you?*
Amanda: *Thanks.*
Susan: *Is this a memory that you are having? Are you trying to tell us what happened to you? Is it your blood?*
[Amanda relates that she hears another female scream.]
Susan: *Did you hurt someone else?*
Amanda: *Where are you?*
Susan: *We are right here; we have not left you.*
Amanda: *What are you not telling us?*
Susan: *We are telling you that you are safe with us. Did you hurt someone? Is that where the blood came from?*
[The flashlight turns on.]
Susan: *Are you trapped down here because you hurt someone?*
[The flashlight and spirit candle turn on at the same time.]
Susan: *Well, we don't want anyone to be hurt.*
Amanda: *You got it.*
Susan: *And we certainly mean no harm to you. We just came down here to talk to you.*
Amanda: *That works.*
Susan: *OK, thank you for talking to us. Tell Amanda goodbye.*
Amanda: *We're angered.*
Susan: *No, we aren't angered.*

At this time, I (Stacey) tapped Amanda on the head to tell her to come out from the headphones since the session was over. It was nearly midnight, and we decided to call it a night. We had more than enough evidence to know that Creek County Courthouse was indeed bustling with spirit activity. Before we left, I did a sweep with my SLS camera and caught a stick figure on the Christmas tree on the first floor. It was then that I learned that all the ornaments on the tree contained photos of victims who lost their lives and whose cases were heard in Creek County. I stared at the tree and reflected on the souls whose lives were lost. It made the car ride home a long and somber one, as I thought back to the many faces of the innocents who lost their lives at the hands of so many. As paranormal investigators, we try to not only seek evidence of the afterlife but also help those who have passed find the peace that they deserve. As always, our hearts and prayers go out to the victims and families of all those lost.

7
The Burnett Mansion

Located one the corner of South Main Street and West McKinley Avenue is a nostalgic, Southern Colonial–style plantation home that once belonged to the Burnett family. Built by Mr. Bolivar Bates Burnett and his wife, Dannie, in 1911, the home is meant to reflect the similar-style home that Burnett was accustomed to seeing back home in Tennessee. Mr. Bates had moved to the Oklahoma area prior to its achievement of statehood with his father, W.J. Burnett, and siblings around the turn of the century. He is listed as bank clerk in the 1900 census. Burnett Sr. worked as a day laborer on a farm until 1869 but eventually advanced himself into the business world when he formed a partnership with Dr. G.L. Brooks and opened a grocery store in Palmersville, Tennessee. His wealth grew along with his property. After the death of his wife, Martha, W.J. Burnett moved his family to Indian Territory and began a new business there as a banker. He passed away a few years later in 1903, leaving his legacy to his children, who chose to stay in Oklahoma and make Sapulpa their home.

Bolivar Bates Burnett was born in Weakley, Tennessee, on January 15, 1875. In his early twenties, just seven short years before Oklahoma achieved statehood, he found his new home in Indian Territory. In 1903, he married Dannie Hughes Ross, and together, they became one of Sapulpa's first socialite families and helped bring development to the town of Sapulpa. The couple had two children, a son, Willliam James Burnett II, and a daughter, Katherine Elizabeth Burnett. Both children would carry on their parents' legacy as prominent citizens of Sapulpa.

Burnett Mansion. *Sapulpa Historical Society.*

Burnett Mansion in the modern day. *Burnett Mansion.*

Mr. and Mrs. Burnett. *Burnett Mansion.*

Like most wealthy men residing in the area known as Indian Territory at this time, Bates Burnett had investments in the oil business. However, that was not his only means of making money at the time. He also owned stock in a banking business, one he shared with his brother Birch Burnett. It was this relation to business that would soon tarnish the "good name" of Bates Burnett.

The Burnett family played a key role in the development of Sapulpa, especially its downtown area. In 1908, the Burnetts helped to build a first-class hotel located on the corner of South Main Street and West Lee Avenue. The new hotel was known as the Saint James Hotel, receiving its name from Bates Burnett's son. The five-story building was said to be one of the finest in the state and cost approximately $100,000 to build; today, that's equivalent to around $3.3 million. The hotel offered one hundred rooms with running water, both hot and cold, as well as electricity and natural gas, private bathrooms in most rooms and even private phone lines. These were luxurious accommodations that were not frequently found during the early statehood of Oklahoma. The hotel remained in operation until 1963, just fifty-five years after its grand opening.

Unfortunately, assisting in the growth and social status of Sapulpa would not be the only historical mark that Mr. Bates would leave on the town's history. As is often seen, with money and power comes scandal, and Mr. Bates was not left untarnished by the role he played in what was considered the first town scandal of Sapulpa.

As previously mentioned, Mr. Burnett also owned stock in a local bank, the Farmers and Merchants Bank, located on the corner of Dewey Avenue and Main Street. In 1913, the Burnett brothers faced legal issues when they were found in contempt of court by Judge Huston for failing to produce the legal documents that showed the banks' books and papers. Both brothers were fined $3,000, the equivalent of $77,000 today. Claims were made that the bank had been looted and the documents taken. However, bank employees who had managed the books stated that when they returned to work, they

South Main Street. *Sapulpa Historical Society.*

found new books where the old ones had once been. Employees and investors also found their names listed among those of the board members without their knowledge or consent, and they said they were never made aware of their assignments or board meetings. It was said that the Burnetts believed the court had no right to compel them to return the books, which might incriminate them should they face criminal charges.

An article posted in the *Sapulpa Times* on January 16, 2022, written by museum curator Racheal Whitney, along with a reference to a previously published article in the *Sapulpa Evening Democrat* from January 15, 1913, stated, "Mr. Patton, a representative of the banking board, testified…one of the many reasons for closing the bank was the large note increase, and thousands of dollars of checks in the drawer as cash items. He read an extensive list of note increases running up into the tens of thousands, nearly all of which went to companies in which the bank was interested." The article also went on to say that Judge Huston reviewed the position of counsel: "He said that as far as the evidence was concerned, it was conclusive that Bates and Birch Burnett had the active management of the bank, and that the books were there when the bank closed. They were responsible for the books and having been ordered to produce them.…There is no contention of burglary or some reasonable excuse; they must produce them." Bail was

Main Street bank. *Sapulpa Historical Society.*

set and paid, but this was not the last of the rulings from Judge Huston. Both brothers also faced ninety days in jail after their convictions. Their reputations in the banking businesses would tarnish their name, but their oil business would once again gain them the respectability they had once known. Bates Burnett passed away on February 4, 1925, in New York City at the age of fifty. His death certificate lists his cause of death as a nasal hemorrhage that developed into lobar pneumonia. However, other sources believe that his real cause of death was suicide after he lost his fortune in the oil business. That story, of course, cannot be validated at this time.

The memories of the Burnett family continue to live on in the grand home they built so many years ago. The mansion currently functions as an event center, hosting various events and weddings. The pure beauty of the craftsmanship inside the home makes it an ideal location. Stacey, Amy, my (Tanya's) daughter Katy and I were all privileged to take a tour of this wonderful location and conduct a quick investigation of the site.

Throughout the home, you can see various pictures of the Burnett family lining the fireplace mantels and adorning the walls. Dark mahogany woodwork lines the windows and doorways. The rich, dark color of the wood can also be seen in the grand staircase and columns leading up to the second floor of the home. Throughout the entire home, you can see the original wallpaper, hand-painted by craftsmen and artists brought over from Italy. The original wooden floors still stretch throughout the home, the exquisite work remaining intact for the past century. Each room is decorated with furniture from the period, but it is not original to the home. However, the small grand piano in the living room area remains original, continuing to claim its rightful place in its grandeur.

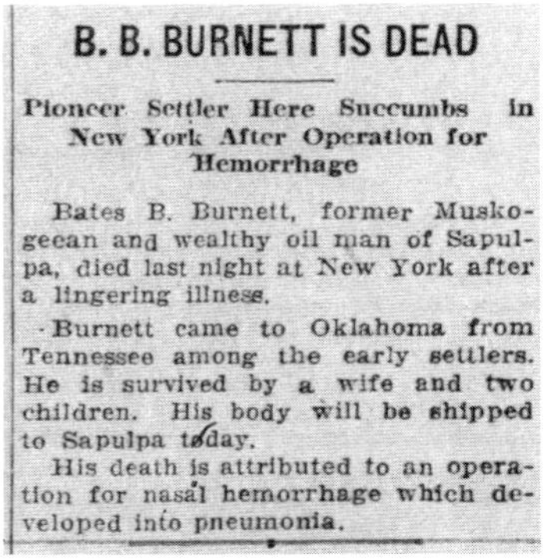

B. B. BURNETT IS DEAD

Pioneer Settler Here Succumbs in New York After Operation for Hemorrhage

Bates B. Burnett, former Muskogeean and wealthy oil man of Sapulpa, died last night at New York after a lingering illness.

Burnett came to Oklahoma from Tennessee among the early settlers. He is survived by a wife and two children. His body will be shipped to Sapulpa today.

His death is attributed to an operation for nasal hemorrhage which developed into pneumonia.

Old newspaper clipping. *Sapulpa Historical Society.*

The mansion is quite extensive in its size. The first level houses the living room, dining area, kitchen, butler's pantry and Mr. Burnett's personal office, with a private exterior door for his business partners and guests to enter. This space still has Mr. Burnett's delicate touch. Artists were commissioned to paint various images of the things Mr. Burnett enjoyed in life, including what appear to be family shields and various poker themes, something he was known to partake in with friends and colleagues. Located just outside of his office is an old push-button call system, which could be used to summon staff from anywhere in the house, should one of the family members need assistance. When you venture upstairs, you come to the first landing of the home, which splits off into two directions. A lovely couch located on the far exterior wall, a piece that once belonged to the Burnett family, remains in place. One direction leads to another set of stairs that lead you up into a large open space that contains the doorways of the family's bedchambers. The smaller staircase leads off to an area that is believed to have been the nursery at one time. The master bedroom contains a large open bathroom, with a claw-foot tub and stained-glassed windows, and a private sitting area that features a fireplace. A beautiful lacy dress that belonged to Mrs. Burnett hangs on display behind a glass showcase, reminding us of what life and fashion were like during that time in history. Just outside the master bedroom in the common sitting area, there is a single door lined by glass windows that leads out to a balcony area overlooking downtown Sapulpa. The Colonial columns continue to accent the balcony as a large glass outdoor chandelier suspended by chains continues to swing softly in the Oklahoma breeze. On the opposite side of the sitting area, you will find another door. This

Burnett family. *Burnett Mansion.*

door, however, does not lead outside. Instead, it leads you deeper into the home as you ascend another staircase leading you into the large open area of the attic.

The attic features several windows and alcove spaces. It is said that this was Elizabeth's space. She could often be found here practicing ballet. Such a large and open space provided ample room for her to practice her arabesque and dégagé techniques. In one small alcove, you can find a small set of wooden benches. The lids open up to a small storage space below, and on one of the lids, you can still see the name Burnett spelled out in pencil, a personal touch left from so very long ago. Our last place to venture into during our tour of the home was the basement area. Another set of stairs, very small in width and length, led our group down into the cold and musky basement of the home. Surprisingly, it was as dark as most basements seem to be. There were ample windows and even an exterior doorway leading into the area. This area was believed to have housed some of the staff, since a full bath was located here, along with various smaller rooms that could have been used as private living quarters at one time. The most intriguing area in the basement was a small arched tunnel, no higher than four feet, which leads off into another adjacent tunnel that appears to branch off into two different directions. Rumor has it that one of the tunnels once led a short distance toward the home of Mrs. Burnett's sister, who fashioned her own home after the Burnett mansion, just on a smaller scale. Upon inspection, one tunnel did appear to have a weaker wall, as a slight breeze could be felt coming through. The concrete floor that leads toward the tunnel still contains the small footprints of a child's boot; it appears they walked on the concrete prior to the completion of the curing process. These footprints do appear slightly different in size and can be seen coming and going throughout the area, once again leaving a special mark and memory in time in this wonderous mansion.

After our initial walk-through was complete, my team and I began to set up equipment to gather our baseline readings in the downstairs area. Amy began receiving high EMF readings immediately in the middle of the living room area, where no electrical outlets could be seen. EMF spikes were also recorded on the piano bench, where no electrical source could be found. Trigger lights were stretched out along the floor leading from the living room area to the dining room. Flashlights were placed in various areas around the grand staircase, as was the ghost candle, to assist us in obtaining equipment responses to the lines of questioning we were about to read out. A REM pod was placed at the top of the stairs, since my attention kept being drawn to that particular location. Within moments, the ghost candle began responding by turning off and on by command. The first spirit we appeared to be talking to was that of a worker who was once associated with the construction of the home. We continued to question it for several minutes, and then another spirit decided to appear at the top of the grand staircase. The REM pod began to sound, and soon, we found ourselves asking questions of the second spirit. It successfully answered our questions using the device. A ghost radio was also able to provide us with some very helpful responses. Our audio recorders were set in various places as well, but the full findings of the audio recordings are still under review. However, we did not require an audio recorder to hear one of the strangest disembodied responses I have heard to date. A loud thumping noise was audibly heard by all five of us who were present that day. It sounded like the drumming of fingers, fingers belonging to the unseen hands of a spirit impatiently waiting for us to either move on or stop our inquiries. The drumming sound lasted for approximately twenty seconds and even repeated itself one more time. Taking the hint, we decided to move on to our second location since our time there was beginning to run short.

For the second session, we decided to split up into two groups to try to cover more ground in the time allotted to us that day. My daughter Katy and I decided to take the second-floor area, containing the living quarters and open seating area, while Stacey and Amy, along with our tour guide, Caitlyn, descended the dark stairwell toward the basement area. Since there have been reports of a woman seen in the upstairs area, particularly by the mirror at the top of the landing, we decided to focus on that area. I set the REM pod in the center of the floor and a flashlight on the chair facing the mirror that both Katy and I felt drawn to. This area gave us a sense of uneasiness and caused the hair on our heads to rise. After several minutes of questioning, we began to get intelligent responses through the REM pod. In the basement below, the rest of our team also had some ghostly interactions. With the use of the spirit candle, they were able to communicate with the spirits that appear to be lingering in the basement area. One EVP that was obtained even stated, "Tell them nothing." It was only after Stacey started reviewing her recordings that she noticed something had turned her recording device off. The device still had battery power, so her only explanation for its failure is that ghostly hands must have played a part in turning it off.

Despite having witnessed multiple events of paranormal activity, our time to leave and head to our next location came. There is no doubt in our minds that ghosts still reside at this historic location, and we are still left with so many questions unanswered. We hope to return here in the near future to seek out the true identities of these spirits and the reasons why so many of them continue linger in this historic mansion—though I certainly can't blame them for doing so.

Currently owned by the Kante Group and managed by the Make Sense Foundation, the mansion now plays host as an event center to help raise funds for the foundation. It's a wonderful foundation that provides scholarships and financial assistance to young women and children in need. This foundation seeks to help those who cannot help themselves, from those living in poverty to those facing abusive home lives.

8

The Sister's House

After our adventures at the Burnett Mansion—and having heard the rumor of a possible sister house to the mansion—I (Stacey) had to go on a little adventure to see if I could locate it. Not only does it exist, but its owners, who have owned the home since 2013, are also some of the loveliest strangers I have ever met. The home is located off Poplar Street, just yards from the mansion. I pulled up in front of the home and found a woman tending the yard. I asked her if she was aware that this house was rumored to the be the sister house to the Burnett Mansion, not just a smaller version of the home but one actually built and owned by Mrs. Burnett's sister. I also discussed the rumor of a tunnel leading from one home to the other and shared with her the small entryway to the tunnel we had found directly across the street. She admitted that while she had never seen the tunnel, she had found what she believed might have been a tunnel at one time. She led me to the part of the house where she found this possible tunnel and showed me a dirt-filled area. She believes it was filled in during the 1970s by another homeowner who was concerned about drug use or parties being held in the tunnel.

The home has many features similar to those of the Burnett Mansion. The front entryway features four large white columns extending up toward the second floor and attic space of the home. Dark mahogany wood lines the walls throughout the home. Beautiful stained-glass windows are featured on each floor of the home. It even includes a separate staircase for the servants and an old-fashioned dumbwaiter system, which, of course, is no longer in use.

One of the home's previous owners married Jimmy Wilson of Jimmy Wilson and the Catfish Band. Live music concerts could often be seen here, but this is not the only fame this home is known for. It also played host to a live broadcast from a radio station when one of the first line tests was being performed to link the original radio station in Bristow to the new location in Tulsa. Another link to fame came when Mike Rowe of *Dirty Jobs*, featured on the Discovery Channel, parked his makeup trailer on the property while filming one of his shows in Sapulpa.

While the current owner admits to not having experienced anything paranormal in the home, she did say that when she turned on a TV in her room, another TV in a different room came on and began flipping through channels, even though it was not the same channel she was trying to switch it to. She stated that she has not had another experience like this. While deadlines did not allow for an investigation of this home, I cannot help but wonder if a child spirit travels back and forth between the homes. Perhaps with future investigations being planned, we might have the opportunity to find out!

9
Creek County Law Office

The Creek County Law Office located at 101 East Lee Avenue resides in an old building that once played host to an array of businesses, including a dental office and a tire shop. The lawyers and staff there have experienced paranormal activity for some time and were welcoming enough to invite us in to investigate their location. Activity started almost immediately for us. Equipment was set up around the rooms and hallways, and Stacey and I (Tanya) split up into two different areas. Still able to hear each other should the other call out, we began our questioning. I was sitting in one of the high-back chairs when I suddenly heard what sounded like footsteps running above my head. I called out to Stacey to ask if anyone was upstairs. She informed me there was no upstairs, this was a single-level building—a fact I had simply forgotten. I asked if that was a spirit and if it could do that again. Immediately I heard the running footsteps again; only this time, they sounded as if they were coming from the wall less than one foot away from me. Luckily, I was filming a live video at the time and was able to catch the sounds on the recording. Stacey informed me one of the staff members said they had heard disembodied footsteps running down the hallways, confirming that what I had just heard had been witnessed before.

We continued with our investigation, receiving several responses to our questions, with the spirits using the tripwires on command to answer them. Knowing we were still extremely limited in time, we decided to do a quick EVP session in one of the back rooms at the end of the hallway. We asked a series of questions, and we were able to obtain their responses on our audio device. We concluded the investigation for the night, but it left us asking more questions than before. Just who were these spirits that resided in this office. Was it even the office that they originated from? Attached to the building, separated by only a brick wall, is another location that houses a group that has gone to other haunted locations around the state. This organization gave me one of the best photographs of a full-body apparition from Guthrie, Oklahoma, many years ago. The building belongs to the American Legion, and in past experiences, I have witnessed various hauntings in many of these lodges around the state. One day, we plan to return to this location and hope to visit the legion hall to see if we can discover which building the spirits actually belong to. Maybe it's simply a wandering spirit, walking throughout the various buildings in historic downtown Sapulpa, continuing to haunt historic Route 66.

10
YOUNGS LAW OFFICE

As Sapulpa is the county seat, it makes sense that a lawyer's office would be easy to find. But what about a lawyer who shares his office with some of Sapulpa's long-forgotten past? One such lawyer can be found at Youngs Law Office. John Young, the current resident and attorney in the building located at Second North Main Street, a corner block along Route 66, is no stranger to Sapulpa. Born and raised here, he continues to call Sapulpa his home. He comes from a long line of lawyers, his grandfather being the one who moved his family to this area many years ago at the beginning of career. He then raised his son to follow in his footsteps, a tradition that was carried down to John. The Youngs took over the ownership of their current building in the 1950s after a large fire threatened their downtown location. In one night, they gathered all their files and began their evacuation to their current location, a building they would inhabit for the next seventy years. The building predates their time there, and in its early years, the building played host to a variety of businesses—some legal and some maybe not so legal. Not everything that occurs in some locations is documented—and often for good reason. This building may be one of those locations.

Young, a former lieutenant colonel in the United States Marine Corps and a highly decorated and well-educated man, greeted us at the door and welcomed us into his historic building. As we sat and spoke about his family's history, he shared with us what history he knew of the building, mainly from the time his family took over its ownership. He took us upstairs to the area that has been reported to have activity. Another paranormal team had previously visited the building and conducted an investigation of their own. They reported finding evidence to support their claim of the building's haunting. Stacey Price and I (Tanya) began our own investigation by setting up various pieces of equipment in the largest open area upstairs. It had once served as a meeting place for a small church group, but it now sat empty, except for a few pieces of furniture scattered around the room. Toward the front of the building, a small curving window cased in aged wood, its paint slowly splintering away, overlooks the street below. As I stood at the window, gazing down toward the pavement, I felt as if I was looking through someone else's eyes, the eyes of a young woman, a woman filled with despair and anguish. A sadness took over me, and it felt as if my heart had suddenly shattered into a million pieces. I shared with Stacey what I had just felt, and we placed some of our equipment around the location. Moments later, it appeared we had contacted a spirit, that of a young lady. We watched as the equipment responded to our series of questions, ecstatic that we were able to make contact. Since we were limited in time that evening and had one more location to visit, we asked if there was anything else that the spirit would like us to know. We then felt large thump that caused me and Stacey to lock eyes. It felt as if a large object, an object heavy enough to shake the entire building, had hit the floor. We had received our answer. We plan to return to this location in the future to see if we can discover the identity of the young lady who stands by the window, gazing out with such a heavy heart. Perhaps one day she can find peace and leave her heartache behind on the historic roadway of Route 66.

11

THE KU KLUX KLAN OF SAPULPA

The year was 1885, and the famous War Between the States had ended. The Civil War was over, but the reconstruction of a torn nation had just begun. The large population of formerly enslaved Black Americans had been set free, but many were left homeless and penniless, with no viable way of supporting themselves or their families. Many began moving north and west in hopes of finding a new home and starting a new life. Many small towns had never seen a Black person, and thanks to propaganda at the time, many fears soon began to develop among the nation's white population, causing unrest and hatred toward a group of people who had already suffered under the hands of injustice. In 1915, a silent film called *The Birth of a Nation* was released. The film, also known as *The Clansman*, is based on a novel by Thomas Dixon (1905). This Hollywood blockbuster not only portrays overt racism against Black Americans and civil rights activists, but it also depicts Black men as the root of all evil, portraying them as lustful, lawless men who harm innocent women. Meanwhile the film depicts members of the Ku Klux Klan as glorified heroes. With the popularity of this movie, many new KKK chapters soon began to take form.

Like many towns around the United States, Sapulpa played host to its own branch of the notorious hate group known as the Ku Klux Klan. Once known as a "sundown town," Sapulpa was not a place to be found walking around after dark if your skin was not white. During this era, another major war had begun, sending many young men and women off to war. Soldiers from all walks of life responded to the country's call as it entered

KKK meeting. *Sapulpa Historical Society.*

World War I. However, it was not only the white citizens who responded to the call. Americans from all walks of life took up arms and fought side by side in the trenches. Once the war ended in 1918 and the soldiers began to return home, many began looking for work once again. Many returned to the Tulsa area, causing a fierce competition in the workforce. Social tensions were at an all-time high, causing an increase in the anti-Black sentiment. As Oklahoma faced economic strains, jobs became harder to find. Crime was at an all-time high, and people were looking for someone to blame.

In Tulsa, Black Americans were thriving and had created a town and lifestyle all their own, best known as the Greenwood District. It eventually gained the nickname "Black Wallstreet." Many white residents of Tulsa, especially those who were facing financial strains of their own, became outraged, believing that a group of "inferior beings" were living a life better than their own. The number of Klan members in Tulsa began to rise, and with them came more anti-Black sentiment. With tensions running high and financial resources becoming depleted, a major event was about to take place just fifteen miles from the heart of Sapulpa in the Greenwood District of Tulsa. From May 31 to June 1, 1921, the Tulsa Riot claimed the lives of innocent men, women and children, leaving an entire district homeless and helpless as they watched their homes, businesses and livelihoods burn to the ground. On June 2, 1922, Sapulpa hosted its first Ku Klux Klan parade. As

Top: Main Street. *Sapulpa Historical Society.*

Bottom: East Dewey Avenue. *Sapulpa Historical Society.*

the men in white walked the downtown street of Devey Avenue, they forever laid claim to part of the city's darkest period.

Sapulpa, like most towns across the state, no longer promotes or glorifies the hate crimes it once did a century ago. This midsize town is a community built on family, farmers and small businesses and is welcoming all who choose to grace it. From its popular Christmas season holiday chute to the famous Route 66 annual event, Sapulpa is a place where family and friends can enjoy a little bit of everything. It's a town for everyone looking for a unique place to visit. As we choose to leave the past in the history books, we choose to turn a new page toward our future, building a community for all and a better place for the next generation.

12
Independent Order of Odd Fellows Building

Several locations around the town of Sapulpa drew my (Tanya's) interest. The weekend we were there happened to be when the town was hosting a founder's celebration. One of the main streets was blocked off and occupied by tents offering crafts and delicious things to eat. Music could be heard on the streets, and friends and families talked and enjoyed the activities. My dear friend Stacey and I headed to a local restaurant to meet the rest of our group for a quick bite before heading to the night's investigation sites. Before arriving at our location, we stopped at one of vendor booths exhibiting information about its business. Stacey was chatting with the owners about their new bagel shop when I happened to notice the picture of a large historic building they were displaying. It happened to be one of the buildings I had been drawn to several weeks before, when I had come to town to do some research. I inquired about the picture, and the owner informed me that it was the site of their business. I immediately asked her about the haunting associated with it. At first, she denied any ghostly activity, as most people would. For some, when they hear you talking about ghosts or hauntings, they look at you with a sideways glance and an implication that you might be crazy—well, they used to, anyway. Today, people are a little more open to sharing their experiences, which makes it easier for others to do the same. When I explained to her who I was and my purpose for being there, she relaxed enough to share a few stories and experiences.

The building they owned used to be the meeting lodge for the Independent Order of Odd Fellows (IOOF). Established in 1806 in New York City, this group consisted of members ranging from actors to boatbuilders. Over the years, lodges and chapters began to form across the United States, and in 1851, IOOF became the first national fraternity to accept both men and women. The only stipulation for membership was that the applicant had to be white. Many of its members belonged to the Ku Klux Klan. While researching their building, the current owners were given copies of pictures showing a KKK meeting that was held in the building—not just in the building but upstairs in what would now be considered their living room, since the owners live above the shop. Much like the Masons, the IOOF had secretive rituals and rites they conducted during meetings. These practices were never spoken of or shared beyond the walls of the meeting places. If only those walls could talk. One mystery that could be solved is that of an old coffin that was found hidden in a secret room in the building. Finding a hidden coffin in any building would pique anyone's interest, but finding the skeletal remains of a small woman in the coffin would blow one's mind. Why would such a thing be hidden in an old lodge? Who was she, and why was she hidden there? These are questions I would love to find the answers to, should I ever be granted permission to investigate the site. We were told that paranormal activity does occur from time to time. Disembodied footsteps can often be heard. One can only imagine what else might be discovered in the secret passageways of the historic Odd Fellows lodge.

13

The Sapulpa Historical Museum

The Sapulpa Historical Museum resides in a three-story brick building, 100 East Lee Avenue, in Sapulpa, Oklahoma. Originally known as the Willis, this location has played host to a series of businesses over the years. The first floor housed several businesses, including the Lee Ave Café, a newsstand, a jewelry store, a piano shop and a Maytag store. The third floor once housed a ballroom and various classrooms for a local business college. The second floor held the old Lee Hotel, which conducted business there from 1910 to 1922. In 1922, the Young Women's Christian Association (YWCA) took over the second floor to offer living quarters to the young women of Sapulpa, and it remained in business until 1968. It was during that same year that the historical society was formed, but it had yet to find a permanent home to house its museum. As a building had to be donated to the nonprofit business, 100 East Lee Avenue was deeded over to the newly formed historical society. From the late 1970s to the early 1980s, the museum opened its doors to the public for the first time, offering its visitors a glimpse into the town's history and helping preserve some items from the town's early years. Today, the museum houses various exhibits and items, along with several pieces depicting the town's timelines and different businesses throughout the years.

Like any other historic location, this building houses its own dark secrets. With years of activity and human emotions seeping deep into the bricks that line the old building's walls, the past continues to live on in the halls of this old building. As the night progressed, we discovered just how much history remained.

East Lee Avenue, Lee Hotel. *Sapulpa Historical Society.*

We set up various pieces of equipment in the front area of the museum. Several small rooms lined the room of the entryway, each depicting a different scene or location from the earlier years of Sapulpa. One of the rooms housed a female mannequin, along with various female wares. I (Tanya) was drawn to this area first, so I headed toward it with a few different pieces of equipment in hand. The moment I crossed the through the door, I felt a shift of energy. Something or someone was with me, despite the fact that I entered alone. I called another member of the team to join me to see if they could feel the energy shift I had just witnessed. After receiving confirmation that she felt the difference as well, we set up the equipment around the small space and began asking a series of questions. We soon began receiving what appeared to be intelligent answers to our questions. The activity continued for several more minutes, but soon, another entity started to make itself known to us. This spirit was just beyond the wall I had been leaning against, in an even smaller room directly behind it. We were both drawn to a small safe that was standing toward the back of the area. We placed an REM pod (an electrical device with a tall antenna that makes a sound should an entity touch it or change the energy in its precise location) on top of the safe. Immediately, we began getting responses from our tool. We conducted a series of questions there as well, using the device as a way for the spirit to answer. The entity made itself known and made sure we knew it was not happy with our presence there. This was the spirit's space and safe, and we were not welcome.

We decided to continue with our investigation, and we headed up to the second floor. I was very curious to see what we might encounter there, since earlier that evening, I had already experienced something that left me a little unnerved. People often ask me what the scariest thing I have ever encountered is or if I get scared doing what I do. At first, there were times I did get scared, but since I have been doing this as long as I have, I don't get scared much anymore. You almost become desensitized with time, so when I find myself a little unnerved at a location, I tend to pay particular attention to it. This location just happened to unnerve me.

Earlier that evening, I was down in the office with Rachel, the museum's curator, while she helped me locate some research I needed. I had sent my team up to the upper floors to start the investigation, saying I would join them shortly. One group had returned while the other was still upstairs. I was told they were on the second floor, so I headed up to retrieve them. I was filming a live feed for Facebook as I went, and I'm glad I was—or at least those watching were, since one of those rare, unnerving moments was soon caught on camera for them. I exited the elevator into the small entryway that was lit with a single light, a light that didn't reach far beyond the archway of the room. As I stepped past its boundaries, I found myself engulfed in darkness—not just any darkness but an eerie darkness, one that sends chills to the very bone. I slowly walked down the long stretch of the hallway, calling out for my team members and expecting someone to answer, but I met only silence. I continued to walk on, thinking perhaps they did not hear my first call. Once again, I tried to call out as I crept deeper into the darkness. Still, I heard no answer. I knew someone was there, but it was not the team members I had originally started out to find. A chill started to climb up my spine as I felt someone or something standing directly in front of me, something that my eyes could not quite see. I decided then that this was not a place I wished to be alone in at that time. I returned downstairs to join the others and noticed that the other group had already returned while I was away. I told them what I had encountered just moments before, so we gathered our equipment and headed back upstairs to see if we could discover what it was that had unnerved me.

We ended up at the very back of the hallway, just past a set of stairs that led down to the floor below. Immediately, the equipment began to sound off all around us. I was sitting on the floor next to the stairwell with my back against the wall when I felt a cold breeze pass. The equipment around me started to alarm to the energy shift I had just felt. A coldness started to take over my right leg. It felt as if a small child had come over to sit on my lap. I told the rest of the group what I was experiencing, and Sheila began taking pictures of the area I was reporting the cold spot from. After reviewing several of the pictures, a foggy white haze can be seen floating just above the area where I felt the presence.

As the investigation continued, our attention was drawn to the stairwell, where we had set up a strand of trigger lights. The lights began to pulse and flash, indicating a presence was near. These were light sequences we had never witnessed before, and they began to emerge from the single strand of lights. Thinking perhaps it was a malfunction with the lights or the wiring on the floor, we gathered the three other stands and laid them along the same area. We used a mel meter to sweep the area to try to locate any possible energy sources, such as wiring, but we couldn't find any. Before long, all four strands of the trigger lights began to light up in various patterns and responses. During this time, we had our ghost radio running as well, and we started receiving responses that appeared to be intelligent answers to our series of questions. Images began to form in my mind, and I asked if someone had hanged themselves from the banister of the stairs. Our guide stated she had not seen any articles on someone hanging themselves there. We continued with our line of questioning. We received several responses related to gambling, along with a few other responses, but there was one response I found rather odd: the word *closet*. The word came up not just once—but twice. So, I jokingly asked if they had "came out of the closet." The trigger lights began to light up all at once. Again, I saw an image and asked the curator if she had known of any deaths that occurred in the building. It was then that the puzzle pieces began to fall into place. The curator suddenly remembered a story she had just come across about a local gambler who had died in the hotel. He was known in town as a gambler who liked to play pool. They had found him one day with a suicide note next to him. The note stated that he wished to be buried the way he was. During the preparation of his body, the morticians discovered the possible meaning behind the note. It was revealed that the person everyone had assumed was a man had actually been born a woman. The death was ruled a suicide due to the discovery of the note, but to many, the wounds suggested otherwise. There were two stab wounds, one to the neck and a second to the chest area. I can barely stand sticking my finger with a needle, so I cannot possibly begin to see how someone could drive a knife into their chest or neck.

Staircase in the old Lee Hotel. *Sapulpa Historical Society.*

Time passed quickly, and we still had another location to investigate before the night was through, so we decided to end there in the hopes of returning to find more answers. We left the museum to head over to the last stop for the night, and even though we had left the museum behind, the question that now plagued my mind would not be so easily left behind. Did this spirit truly die by suicide, or were they perhaps a victim of an unsolved murder from decades before? Is that why the spirit has not passed on? Could they simply be waiting for the truth to be told so they can finally rest in peace? I look forward to the day we return to the museum to see if we can uncover the possible truth that may be hidden within the walls of the old hotel, where the restless spirits still wander the halls, looking for something they may have been denied so many years ago: justice.

Our Return to the Sapulpa Historical Museum

One of the joys I've (Stacey) had when taking skeptics into the museum to investigate is seeing them walk out scratching their heads at what they witnessed. As paranormal investigators and local authors, we are often asked to be guests for various news stations and do interviews for radio stations and newspapers. The Sapulpa Historical Museum is a wonderful place for us to take guests. This location has always held a special place in our hearts and in those of the people who work there. It's always guaranteed to provide you with a dose of paranormal activity.

A reporter for the local newspaper reached out to us with hopes of writing an article on some of the local haunted locations. We decided to invite him to investigate with our team. He and his wife joined us for a night of investigations at the museum, and as always, the museum did not disappoint.

Once inside, we showed them the equipment and explained some of the science behind it, such as the SLS camera. We showed them what images would show up when you pointed it at a mannequin or a live person; when it detects a person, it shows the image of a stick figure. However, when it was pointed at a bookshelf where activity was felt, a stick figure could be seen hanging off of it, leaving no explanation for what could have caused the reading.

That night, team member Lee Tanner and I were sitting on a bench near the bathrooms on the first floor, giggling softly, while the other investigators were upstairs. We noticed someone moving by the wall on the other side. I apologized for laughing out loud, thinking we had disturbed another investigator's session. But when I received no response, I shined my flashlight toward the area where we had noticed the movement, only to notice that there was no one there. I quickly grabbed my equipment to try to figure out who had just come out of the wall. Having seen multiple full-body apparitions in the past, I realized I had just witnessed one again. It isn't something you see every time you go out, especially at a new site, so when you do see one, it can be pretty spectacular.

Another group was doing an EVP session when they suddenly heard water coming from a bathroom down the hall. Two of the investigators went in search of the sound, and what they discovered sent chills down their spine. Not only was the water on, but they were the only people on the floor when this incident occurred.

Once again, this location did not fail to provide us with some amazing experiences, and it left a newspaper reporter scratching his head about what he had just experienced at one of Sapulpa's most haunted locations.

This location is not only a wonderful place to take newspaper reports, but it's also the type of location where you can take a news crew, like we did one night, to film a Halloween special for a Tulsa news crew. On this particular night, Tanya and I set up our equipment as the cameraman readied his camera and equipment for a night of filming. One of our first locations was an upstairs room that held artifacts from a YWCA, where only ladies shared housing. As we began our session in the room using a portal, we began getting messages that said the spirit was female and attached to one of the items near the vanity in the room. As we tried to focus on what the spirit was trying to tell us, a loud noise came from the direction where the cameraman was standing. We turned to see the light we had just securely attached to his camera lying on the floor. Immediately, Tanya picked up on a female spirit that was not happy a male was in her room, so out of respect, we decided to move out of the room and into the hallway area. As we continued our quest to get information on who we were speaking to, we decided to try to use a few other devices to get more evidence. Using the motion sensor cat balls on the floor and our tripwire, the spirits soon began responding to our line of questioning. When we asked if they were responsible for the cameraman's light hitting the floor, the cat ball immediately lit up. We then asked if it had caused the light to hit the floor because a male was in a females' room. We got another positive response light on the cat ball. Throughout the remainder of the night, the spirits continued interacting with us, allowing us to glimpse into what their life had like been so many years ago. We thanked them for their time in the hopes of meeting with them again when we return to the haunted Sapulpa Historical Museum.

14

Waite Phillips–Barnsdall Filling Station Museum

Located on the corner of Water Street and Lee Avenue in Sapulpa is a small filling station better known as the Waite Phillips–Barnsdall Filling Station Museum. It is a small historical gas station that one might have seen while traveling along Route 66 prior to the construction of the turnpike. Waite Phillips opened this location in 1922 as an independent oil and gas company. In 1930, he sold his small business and joined his brothers Frank and E.L. Phillips in establishing the Phillips Petroleum Company. He spent two decades building his fortune in oil. In 1920, Waite Phillips bought more than three thousand acres of land near Cimarron, New Mexico, with dreams of becoming a rancher. In 1938, Waite founded the Southwestern Art Association. This association was later gifted his Tulsa estate, the Villa Philbrook. The villa later became the Philbrook Museum of Art.

Today, this historic filling station sits as a testament to his meager beginnings and his accumulation of wealth and success. Now part of the Sapulpa Historical Museum, this location displays two historic cars from Phillips's period, along with memorabilia from that time. During one night of investigating some of the various buildings owned by the museum, we decided to investigate the old filling station to see what possible paranormal activity might still be lingering there.

We gathered around the tables, each taking a seat. Various pieces of equipment had been set up around the two rooms in the hopes the spirits would interact with them that evening. We did not have to wait long. As we began asking our series of questions, one of the flashlights that had been

Top: Barnsdall Service Station. *Sapulpa Historical Society.*

Bottom: Historic cars on display. *Tanya McCoy.*

sitting on a nearby glass display case began to lighting up and turning off with each question and command. "If you're a male, can you touch one of the flashlights please?" The flashlight on the case turned on. "Thank you. Can you turn it back off again so we can ask another question?" The light quickly went out. "Are you attached to this location?" Once again, the flashlight turned on. During this time, noises could be heard coming from the room adjacent to the one we were currently in. The plasma light in the other room also began lighting up. In that room, the two classic cars stood side by side, and various pieces of old tools were stored in various locations. Again, our attention was drawn toward the glass case that stood against the wall in front of us. As we continued with our questioning, we asked if the spirit we were talking to was attached to something in or around the glass case. Various old pictures hung about on the wall, while several others were displayed behind the glass. In response to our question, the flashlight lit up once again. With activity occurring in both rooms, we soon began to believe that we were possibly speaking to two different spirits. After a quick Estes session, we decided to move over into the smaller building located next to the car bays and the room we were currently in.

The other location once served as the small office of the gas station area where the old pumps once stood. There, we began asking questions of another spirit that appeared to join us. This spirit appeared to be a woman, but she did not appear to belong to this site. Instead, she informed us that she was the spirit who stayed in the law office across the street, where Stacey and Racheal (our other team member) had once worked. She validated this fact by saying Racheal's name and admitting to being the ghost that watches over the candy bowl in their office. After a few more questions were asked and answered, we decided it was time to end our session at this location, as we still had one more location to investigate that night. We said goodbye to the spirits there and thanked them for their time as we packed up and headed down the street to investigate the Sapulpa Fire Museum. But we assured them that we would see them again in the near future.

15

Sapulpa Fire Museum

Located on the same block as the Sapulpa Historical Museum is another location that serves as the Sapulpa Fire Museum. Various pieces of firefighting equipment that were used in previous years are housed in this building. You can also see groups of photos showcasing some of Sapulpa's most horrific fires. In the black-and-white photos, you can see multiple locations, including a historic church and an entire hotel, that were reduced to mere rubble. The pictures cannot do justice to the challenges these brave souls faced while on duty. Though this building never played the part of an actual fire station, it contains many objects that played such a vital role in the fire personnel's daily lives.

Two of Sapulpa's historic fire trucks are located here. The smaller truck serviced the town of Sapulpa from the 1930s to the 1960s. The larger truck served as a ladder truck for the department and lay witness to one of Sapulpa's most tragic accidents, the death of a beloved firefighter, Sapulpa's first fireman to lose his life while trying to save others.

Robert A. Estes passed away in the early morning hours of April 9, 1976. Estes had been operating the nozzle of the hose while battling a burning building when the aerial ladder collapsed with him on it. Loved by family, friends and coworkers, this brave hero is honored and remembered to this day for his heroic actions and for paying the ultimate price while attempting to save others.

Being a first responder carries a lot of responsibility and can often leave an emotional impact on those who are active in the field. Even the events

Old Sapulpa Fire House. *Sapulpa Historical Society.*

nurses encounter in their line of work can often leave them traumatized, and they carry the weight of those events on their shoulders for the rest of their lives. When it comes to paranormal energy or probable causes for paranormal activity, human emotions often play an important role in creating energy shifts and are a possible reason for these occurrences. So, it should be no surprise to learn that a fire station, hospital, prison or police

Fire trucks. *Tanya McCoy.*

station has reports of paranormal activity. Although this location has never been an actual fire station, the personal items and equipment stored here can hold paranormal energy, energy that my team and I (Tanya), along with the museum curator who was with us, were soon witnesses to.

Our investigation began like most others; team members scanned the room for areas with high EMF levels that might interfere with our equipment readings and found locations to place various pieces of equipment, such as our flashlights, cat balls, EMF devices and spirit candles. Once our equipment was set in place, our EVP session began. We began by asking questions like "Can you tell us your name?" and "Did you used to work on one of these trucks?" We immediately began getting responses to both of our questions. The flashlight that we had was sitting on one of the trucks, and it began going off and on, simultaneously with the spirit candle, in response to our questions. This led us to believe that we were speaking to someone who was once associated with the equipment housed there. The Geoport (a device that is supposed to work using three different energy sources that it then transmits to into an audio response) was set up next. We were hoping to capture more evidence to help with our investigation.

Old Sapulpa fire truck. *Tanya McCoy.*

Multiple responses were soon obtained as our line of questioning continued. As the hour grew late, we decided to end our investigation, content that we had obtained enough evidence and witnessed enough activity to conclude that this location was indeed haunted—not by any evil spirit or entity but by a few who seem to carry on their diligent care of watching over the citizens of their hometown of Sapulpa.

A special note from us to all the emergency personnel who risk their lives daily to protect ours: we send you our love, thanks and prayers for your safety as you face each day in the field.

16

THE SAPULPA HOSPITAL

One of the locations I (Stacey) was advised to visit was Sapulpa's local hospital. A detective had advised me that I needed to speak to the night nurses, as it was rumored that the ghost of Dr. Bartlet was still visiting patients. I had no idea how I was going to accomplish that task until one lucky—or unlucky, if you ask my husband—night we had to make a rush to the emergency room. Upon checking my husband in for urgent care and being reassured he was not in danger of dying, I proceeded to take out my phone and open the microphone to begin recording in the room. I wanted to see if I could capture any spirits who might want to chat. I mean, when life gives you lemons, you may as well make lemonade. While waiting in the emergency room with my husband, I asked the spirits to speak into the microphone on my phone, and I captured a very clear response saying, "What do you use it for?"

When I learned they wanted to keep him overnight, I admittedly was a little too happy about the opportunity to spend the night at a haunted hospital. How awesome is that? With glee in my heart—and, as always, a flashlight and cat balls in my purse (I mean doesn't everyone carry these?)—we were whisked away to our room on the second floor of the hospital.

After getting my husband settled in, I did one EVP session, and after enjoying some spirit candle action and EVP sessions, I decided to step out of the room and head down toward the nurse's station. One sweet nurse who was kind enough to grant me an interview shared with me that there are TVs that will come on by themselves, and in one room, the TV will switch to a specific channel. She also told me that another nurse saw someone back in surgery when nobody was doing any surgeries. In one room, a long-term patient who passed away has evidently decided to stay there. Oftentimes, other patients have reported seeing their bathroom lights turning off and on by themselves while no one is there. Many nurses don't like to go to the back side of the hospital alone. In fact, when one of them has to go back there, they will buddy up and take another along with them just so they don't have to go alone. Hospitals are notorious for being haunted. With the numbers of injuries, deaths and other events that take place there, it's no wonder there are so many hospitals being haunted to this day.

17

The Euchee Mission Boarding School

In 1891, the Presbyterian Mission Board, along with the help of Samuel Brown, Noah Gregory, Henry Land and William Sapulpa, began planning a school for the local Euchee Indians in the Sapulpa area. The money needed was provided by the tribal funds, and the school would serve both the Creek and Euchee children. The large campus-like facility was located on forty acres of land, allowing for the campus to grow.

Originally, the facility was under the direction of the Presbyterian Mission Board, but in 1897, the Creek Nation took over the supervision of the school until 1907. From 1907 to 1925, the school's supervision was transferred over to the Office of Indian Affairs. From 1925 to 1929, the school functioned as a boy's school, and the integration of the older students into the Sapulpa Public School System began.

When the school's doors first opened in the fall of 1894, it had the capacity to house 80 students. Since the school was co-ed at that time, it had two dormitories and one three-roomed schoolhouse. Since agriculture was a huge part of the Euchee culture, planting and maintaining a large garden was part of the school's curriculum. When the institution transitioned into an all-boys school in 1925, there were 110 students attending, which led to the construction of more buildings on the site. The school continued to function as an all-boys institution until 1947.

In 1947, the remaining students were transferred into the Sapulpa Public School System. The city purchased the land, and the Euchee Mission Boarding School was demolished. Later, the land was used to house the

Top: Old Indian School. *Sapulpa Historical Society.*

Bottom: Euchee Boarding School, Sapulpa, 1891. *Vinson Lackey, Tulsa: Gilcrease Museum, https://live-gmcd.pantheonsite.io/object/011419.*

Sapulpa High School, a junior high and an elementary school. The high school remains there today. However, it is reported that it will face demolition in 2026.

There have been many reports of paranormal activity within the walls of the current Sapulpa High School, whispered rumors of shadow figures seen walking the corridors and disembodied voices and laugher. Students have reported stories they were told by the janitors who work alone in the building at night and shared the eerie feelings they experienced while walking alone down the long dark corridors.

Throughout the state of Oklahoma, we have many Indian Missionary Boarding Schools, and many remain haunted to this day. The forced removal of the Native children from their homes was not a gentle process. The children were often treated very cruelly and denied the religion or beliefs of their own culture. They were forced into a new way of life; their hair was cut, their language was prohibited and their teachings were condemned. Severe punishment was given if the rules were not followed, and many children passed away under the care of their supervisors. This left a dark mark on history, and the presence of paranormal activity stains the land.

In 1998, the Oklahoma Historical Society erected a stone marker where the Euchee Boarding School once stood. The area that once housed the garden maintained by the Euchee and Creek students now plays host to the Sapulpa High School football field. Yuchi languages and culture have faded away with time, but through the efforts of a few, the culture still lives on and is being taught in a small Yuchi facility just outside of Sapulpa. It is called the Yuchi Language Project, and it offers a chance for Yuchi heritage to live on through teaching the youth the history of their ancestors. For more information, please visit www.yuchilanguage.org.

18
THE SAPULPA LIBRARY

Libraries have always held a special place in my (Tanya's) heart, even when I was a kid. As a child, I had difficulty reading. It was not until almost thirty years later, when I discovered that my youngest child was dyslexic, that I realized the issues I had back then were related to my own disability, one I had to struggle with to overcome. My older sister was an avid reader, and I remember being jealous of how easy reading a book was for her. I would always struggle to get through one. Now, forty years later, I am writing them. It is quite amazing how marvelously our brains can be trained and rewired when we work to overcome a challenge. It was my love of books and the adventures in them that drove me to become an avid reader. I guess that is why libraries and bookstores are so precious to me. There is nothing quite as special as walking along the stacks of an old library or enjoying the smell of the worn pages and ink that linger there. However, at times, it is not just history that lives on between the books and shelves of a library. Sometimes, we can find a few extra bits of history staying around—and by that, I mean ghosts.

Located at 27 West Dewey Avenue in Sapulpa, there is a two-story red brick building that currently houses the Sapulpa Library. Designed by architects H.O. Valeur & Co. and constructed in 1917 by C.E. Kodane and L.O. Lytle with a special library grant provided by Andrew Carnegie, the Sapulpa Library opened its doors for the first time. Today, the library resides on the second floor of the building, while the genealogy department resides on the first floor alongside a few meeting rooms reserved for special events.

Carnegie Library. *Sapulpa Historical Society.*

Libraries are known for being quiet places, and visitors are instructed to keep the noise down to a bare minimum. Since the library has such a well-known history, one can only imagine how pleasantly surprised we were to find this particular location was not going to be quiet the night we investigated there.

It seems that the ghosts of the Sapulpa Library like to make themselves known to both staff and guests. When the staff were asked what paranormal activity they had witnessed in the past, they were more than happy to share their own experiences with us. On various occasions, the staff has witnessed a ghostly presence in various shadow forms in the stairwell area. On another occasion, a group who had gathered downstairs in the Frank Hall Auditorium reported hearing the sounds of ghostly footfalls running above them on the second floor when no one was there. After gathering this information, Stacey decided to leave a voice recorder in the genealogy department to obtain some possible EVPs. Leaving the device to continue recording, Stacey told the spirits, "Please feel free to come forward and chat," as the group left to move on to another area of the building. When she reviewed the recording, she heard what appeared to be a large crash of some type followed by a ghostly whisper saying, "Help me." Unfortunately, it was the only EVP captured in that location at that time, but it was a simple foreshadowing for what lay in store for the team the rest of the night.

Near the old entrance to the library, you can find a few tables, chairs and even a couch to sit on. This became our first investigation site for the evening. After scanning the area with our EMF meters to try to detect

East Dewey Avenue. *Sapulpa Historical Society.*

any wiring or anything that might cause our equipment to have a false reading and discovering our baseline reading, we sat down to begin our investigation. The first thing we discovered was the possible presence of an entity on one of the chairs near us, as we had a spike in readings on our K2 meter. As we began our line of questioning, we started to obtain various responses from our spirit candle, flashlights and cat balls, which had been left in various places around the area. While we were conducting this part of the investigation, the daughter of one of the staff members called to share her own experience at the library. While on speakerphone, she related her story. In 2019, she had been downstairs in the room adjacent to the boiler room while her father was setting up tables by the kitchen area. It was a dark and creepy night, and her dad began to tell her about the strange occurrences her mother had witnessed while working there late at night. He claimed that her mother would often hear noises coming from downstairs when no one else was in the building. He had hopes of scaring his young daughter, but little did he know that a ghost had a few tricks up its own sleeves. After making a few more jokes about the place being haunted, they began to hear a series of strange knocks coming from the other side of the door, the same door that divides the stage and kitchen, the location they were currently in—alone. With that, the daughter decided it was time to leave the area, and she did not look back as she quickly ascended the stairs to the safety of her mother.

During our next session, we decided to use the Geoport, since it resembles an old radio. Using this device, we hoped to obtain more answers to the vast number of questions we were asking. Stacey began asking if there were any spirits present and if they could give us their name. The first response we received was "Mary Russell." Other names we heard that night were Andy, Ace Pellington, Chris and Bobby Lee. The following is a rendition of the Geoport activity from that session.

GEOPORT SESSION

You're mocking me.
[Who smells?] **Reply:** *Death.*
What's up?
Go to the light.
I don't know.
And then the angel cometh.
[How many souls are here with us?] **Reply:** *Ten.*
It just came to me now!
Good job, man! Thank you!
Get out of here!
We have them. We'll get them.
Believe.
Discover me.
Silence!
It's a long way from home.
[Do you like having an audience?] **Reply:** *It's boring.*
Help!
Is Kelly here?
Stacey.
Diane.
Hide.
[We explained to the spirits that they can talk through the radio.] **Reply:** *It can talk.... That's freaky!*
People hear me.

Leave!
Who is this?
Ask Stacey.
Quiet!
Don't let them.
Take a break.
Please.
Yes, that's her drawing.
I don't want you stressing him out.
You think?
You big slut.
Ask her.
Behind you.
[And this is probably my (Stacey's) favorite response of the night.] *We were expecting you.*

The entire night was active with flashlights and cat balls lighting up and unexplained knocks and recorded sounds. Based on our activity level, we cannot wait to go back again.

No one is sure just how many spirits may still reside in the Sapulpa library, but one thing is for certain, they all appear to be pretty happy there. After all, why wouldn't they be? It appears the librarians there are continuing to take excellent care of both the living and the dead. So, next time you visit your local library, make sure to not only keep your eyes on your reading; you might also take a quick look around. You never know who—or what—you might see lingering in the pages of the past.

19

The Sapulpa Chamber of Commerce

Located just a few steps away from the Route 66 Vintage Market on the corner of Dewey Avenue and Water Street is the office of the Sapulpa Chamber of Commerce. One of the oldest buildings remaining in the downtown area off historic Route 66, this two-story brick building has graced the streets of Sapulpa since 1908. Known as the IOWA building, originally built in 1905 but having to be rebuilt due to a large fire in 1908, it continues to house some of Sapulpa's Main Street business to this day. This location once housed a hardware store, a tailor shop, an osteopath doctor's office, an attorney's office and several others throughout the years. However, the most intriguing business this building once housed was another one of Sapulpa's infamous bordellos, and this is where our story begins.

After speaking with the chamber of commerce, we were granted access into the building to conduct a small paranormal investigation. I (Tanya) had just been contacted by a local news reporter from Fox 23 out of Tulsa to film a short new piece for my latest book, *Oklahoma's Haunted Route 66*. I had asked Stacey to join me, and we met up with the news crew to conduct our interview at the Sapulpa Historical Museum. After filming our A roll and sitting down for our interview, we decided to meet up again to film B roll. The reporter and cameraman planned to follow Stacey and me through two of the locations in Sapulpa. The news reporter, Julia Gorman, along with her assistant, followed us through the first location as they filmed us investigating the museum. They got to experience some paranormal activity firsthand when one of the spirits knocked the light off the top of the camera

Historic downtown Sapulpa. *Sapulpa Historical Society.*

while the camera operator was holding it. After the filming was completed at the museum, we drove over to meet them at the chamber of commerce building, where we were allowed access to continue our investigations.

With the doors locked behind us, the four of us began to climb the stairs leading us up to the second floor. We walked around the area, familiarizing ourselves with the building's layout. When we reached the top of the stairs, we were greeted by a small landing that led us back toward the front of the building. A few small rooms line the wall, lit by only the streetlights that line the dark and quite Dewey Avenue below. As we turned the corner, we were greeted by another small hallway that led us toward the back of the building. Each side of the hall is also lined with small individual rooms, each housing their own private sink. Toward the very back of the hall is a small dark room that houses an old bathroom area. This particular area would prove to be one of the more active areas for our investigation that night.

Stacey and I began to set up equipment in various locations around the upstairs area. With no doors attached at any of the doorways, we were left with a clear view through several of the rooms, which lead into one another. As the film crew prepared their own equipment, our equipment began to sound off in various locations around the area. I noticed what appeared to be the dark shadow of a man standing just a few doors away looking back at us. He appeared to be dressed in early Western-style clothes as he paced back and forth in the room just fifteen feet away. We began asking him questions, and he began responding using our REM pod and flashlight. A second REM pod began to sound out just a few doors down in the bathroom area, and it continued to sound throughout the rest of the investigation. Disembodied footsteps could be heard shuffling around, despite all four of us sitting on the floor. There was no one else in the building with us that night—well, at least no one else who was currently living. We soon began experiencing temperature changes as the activity we were experiencing began to ramp up. We decided to conduct an Estes session in which I attempted to gather answers about whoever was still haunting the building. We obtained multiple responses that night. Our first word was *captain*, followed by *exorcism* and *evil*. Other disturbing words continued to come through, such as, *hurry*, *away*, *get out*. We even received questions, such as, "Who's there?" And this was followed by, "We're alive." When we asked the spirit to give us its name, we received the response, "Anna and Rose." We were also given the name Jim. Apparently, Jim was the spirit who did not want us around. We asked Jim if he wanted us to leave. His reply was simple. "Yes! Yes! Yes! Now!" This was followed by another spirit replying, "All dead."

I also saw a faint figure of a woman there. She appeared to be in her late teens or early twenties. She wore a long, lacy, cream-colored gown and she had her hair up in a loose, large bun that extended around the base of her head. When I first looked at her face, she seemed sad, just staring back at me. Then her face suddenly began to change, as if she was aging quickly; her cheeks and eyes sank inward, giving her face the appearance of a skeleton. Around that time, a large bang was heard downstairs. Convinced someone was trying to either open the door or unlock it to come in, Stacey ran downstairs to see what was going on. The door remained locked, and as she opened it to take a look outside, she saw no one in sight. The streets remained dark and empty. As she returned upstairs, we decided to call it a night, as it appeared the spirits were becoming restless with our questioning. The room felt very busy to me, and it seemed like several spirits were walking back and forth throughout the area. I told Stacey that I felt as if I could see both men and women traveling from this upstairs area and entering through the wall to the building adjacent to it. Stacey then informed me that there had once been a doorway there that connected the two buildings. That doorway led over to the top of the other side, where an illegal gambling ring had been rumored to exist. The only thing that existed there now was a brick wall where the doorway once stood.

As we began to head downstairs, a small knothole in the wood flooring drew my attention. Curiously, I knelt down on the floor and shined my flashlight into the small peephole. I noticed something peculiar hidden between the boards of the wood flooring. I placed my finger through the knothole and easily lifted the small plank. Inside, I found a small bone and a small black button. Both appeared to be very old and hidden away there together. I quickly removed the items and took them downstairs, where Stacey and the ladies from the chamber of commerce were waiting for me. I showed them what I had found, and we returned to the site. I explained to them how I was drawn to that particular board in the floor where I had found the items. I was given the two items to add to my haunted collection for the Haunted Route 66 Museum I plan to open.

Over a year has passed since the discovery of the button and bone beneath the wooden floorboards of the old IOWA building. I felt at the time that there was a significance to the items and how they were found. I recently discovered that there is actually a divination practice called "bone casting" in which one can use bones along with small objects, such as buttons, shells or charms, to cast a spell. There is also another use for these types of items in Magick (witchcraft, not magic performed in magic shows). These items can be used in love spells, protection spells, money spells and even Black Magick. The reason these two items to might have been placed together so many years ago is unknown, but finding this little bit of history that remained hidden for long made the hunt well worth it.

20

The Heart of Route 66 Vintage Market

Nestled along the historic brick-paved streets of Sapulpa is a quaint little antique shop called the Heart of Route 66 Vintage Market. Located at 105 East Dewey Avenue, this three-story building spans across a large space and has taken part in Sapulpa's long past. From a speakeasy to a law firm, this building has seen it all. Even Hollywood has laid claim to making an appearance here when the upstairs area was used to film a scene from the movie *Rumble Fish,* a 1983 film directed by Francis Coppola, starring famous actors Matt Dillon and Mickey Rourke. The grandeur of Hollywood may have drizzled away, but the uniqueness of this building still exists. Now housing the Heart of Route 66 Vintage Market, this building plays host to an array of goods, making it easy for potential clients to find that unique gift for their special someone. Vintage Market is the kind of place where you can walk the entire store over and still not see everything it has to offer. As you wander through the various alcoves and aisles, you will find a vast array of goods from decades and centuries past. Items like furniture pieces, books, dolls and war memorabilia—not to mention a few hand-crafted items—can be found in every nook and cranny. But the uniqueness of this location doesn't end there. There are some things that you might find that aren't simply displayed on a shelf. You might find yourself stumbling on something or someone you might not have expected to see at all.

Vintage Market. *Tanya McCoy.*

As this building has such a long, checkered history, it should come as no surprise that many spirits wander here. Most visitors are allowed to walk only in the areas on the first floor and a small portion of the second floor, where the various vendor goods are displayed. However, Tanya and I (Stacey), along with a few of our team members, were allowed to investigate the rest of the building to see for ourselves the paranormal activity that resides there.

As we ascended the stairs to the mezzanine, we felt a heaviness start to overcome us. The area is now used to store various furniture pieces, items and movie posters from years gone by. An uneasiness began to take over both Tanya and me. We began to feel dizzy as we reached the top of the stairs, unsure of what awaited us there. Tanya even felt threatened as she attempted to descend the stairs. She stopped and braced herself on each side of the wall in an attempt to steady herself, feeling as if an unknown force would soon push her from behind. Her fears were soon rationalized, as the word *threaten* came up in a session later that evening. While we don't know what spirit might have been trying to communicate to us, we believe it was some sort of warning. Choosing to play it safe, we warned the other investigators to use their hands to brace themselves by holding onto the wall while going up and down the stairs—just in case something menacing did reside there.

There are times during our investigations that our clients wish to observe, and we allow it. That night, it was the spirits that asked them to join us. Various pieces of equipment were used during this investigation, including a Geoport. The following is the transcript from that session.

GEOPORT TRANSCRIPT

Stacey: *Who's the female?*
Geoport: *Susan.*
Stacey: *We brought Mike.*
Geoport: *It's him.*
Stacey: *It's Mike; it's him. What do you want to tell him?*
[The cat ball lights up.]
Stacey: *Do you like the cat ball?*
[The cat ball lights up.]
Geoport: *Look.*
Stacey: *Do you have a message for Mike?*
Geoport: *Yup.*
Stacey: *Can you tell him your message?*
Geoport: *The hat.*
Stacey: *Are you talking about Archie?*
Geoport: *Archie.*
Geoport: *Yup.…Stacey* [whisper].
Stacey: *You can talk to me.*
Geoport: *No.…Who's talking* [in a female voice]*?*
Stacey: *I'm Stacey.*
Stacey: *We have Archie and Mike here. Who else do you want to talk to?*
Geoport: *Two more* [in a female voice].
Stacey: *Do you just want everyone up here?*
Geoport: *Yeah, there is.…I can't.*
Stacey: *What was the message about the hat?*
Geoport: *Hmmmm* [in a female voice]*.…Just wait.*
Stacey: *What are we waiting on?*
Geoport: [Low growl.]
Stacey: *Whose horse is that? What's the little boy's name that comes up here?*
Geoport: *Stacey* [whisper]*.…I don't know* [in a female voice].
Stacey: *It's Stacey again. What did you want to tell me?*
Geoport: *Stacey.…You.*
Stacey: *Can you touch that cat ball over there again?*
Geoport: *Stacey.*
Stacey: *I'm here.*
[The flashlight comes on.]

Geoport: *Me.*
[The candle comes on.]
Geoport: *What is it* [in a female voice]*?...Say it.*
[Amanda identifies two entities having a conversation.]
Geoport: *Jack.*
Stacey: *Is Jack in the army?*
Geoport: *Say it.*
Stacey: *Tell me if Jack was in the army.*
Geoport: *Seven* [in a female voice].
[Stacey identifies there are seven humans upstairs listening to this session.]
Geoport: *Seven* [in a male voice]....*Seven* [in a male voice].... *Go back.*
Stacey: *Where do you want us to go back to?*
Geoport: *Back.*
Stacey: *Back where?*
[The flashlight comes on.]
Geoport: *Seven.*
Stacey: *How many spirits are here with us?*
Geoport: [A creepy whisper.]
Stacey: *Tell me how many spirits there are here.*
Geoport: *Four.*
Stacey: *How many souls are up here? Can you yell at it?*
Geoport: *Eight....Seven*
[Amanda identifies that underneath the answer, there is a whisper that "doesn't sound right."]
Geoport: *Eight....I don't know* [in a female voice]....*It's them* [in a male voice].
Susan: *Who are they?*
Stacey: *What is the female trying to say? I need her to speak louder.*
Geoport: *I'm here* [in a female voice].
Stacey: *Let me talk to the female....You boys need to step back and let the female talk.*
Geoport: *Talk*
Susan: *Say, yes, we want to talk.*
Geoport: *Go* [in a female voice].
Stacey: *Do you want us to leave?*
[The Geoport dies, and the session ends.]

We conducted two Estes sessions that evening. I (Stacey) participated in the first one; the second was conducted by Amanda, another team member. Using a spirit box and noise-canceling headphones, the Estes sessions began. After completing her session, Amanda's face appeared red, as if she suffered from a slight sunburn, despite it being nighttime and the fact that our investigation was held inside. When it was my turn to do the Estes session, I lay the spirit box on my chest and leaned back in a comfortable chair. Immediately, our temperature gages began to go off, a warning sign that alerts us to sudden increases in temperature. It felt as if I had stuck my face in a hot oven, despite no heat sources being located in the room. With the knowledge that a large, historic fire had taken place in the downtown Sapulpa area, I wondered if Amanda might have been witness to a paranormal phenomenon and could feel the heat of the fire that burned down the building many years ago. When it comes down to all I have seen in the paranormal world, anything is possible. During the two sessions, our audio recorders were set to document all the sounds in the room. The following is the transcript recorded from my Estes session. During these sessions, it is important that the person going "under" cannot hear the others who are asking questions. This ensures that the audio heard through the device is not tainted or contaminated by the questioners.

STACEY'S ESTES SESSION

Susan: *All right, be ready with your answers, because Stacey is going to put some earplugs in and she's* [not] *going to be able to hear you talk.*

Stacey: *If you are talking, I can't hear you.*

Susan: *OK, good.…Can you hear me now? Can you hear me now. No.* [No answer.] *OK, that's good.*

Stacey: *Let's go ahead and start.*

Susan: *OK.*

[Silence.]

Geoport: *Who's this?* [It sounds *very much* like a person with a British accent.]

Susan: [Laughs] *That's a yes. Stacey has her earplugs in, and she will be able to hear you through the device that she's listening to. So, can you…oh, confirmation we've got the light. The candle lit up. Can you tell us your name?*

Stacey: *Trouble.*

Susan: *Are you going to be causing trouble?* [The spirit candle lights up.] *Yes, OK. Is that you being funny?*

Stacey: *Attic.*

Susan: *Is there trouble in the attic? Is there something we need to be aware of?*

Stacey: *Work.*

Susan: *Did she say she works? All right, is there something we need to worry about? Tell me more about the trouble in the attic.*

Stacey: *Jennifer.*

Susan: *OK, who is Jennifer?* [Directed to store owner] *Do you know a Jennifer?*

Store owner: *I have a vendor named Jennifer.*

Susan: *Oh! What level is she on?*

Owner: *She's on this* [level] *right here.*

Susan: *OK, she's on this level.*

Stacey: *Help.*

Susan: *Does Jennifer need help?*

Store owner: *Is Jennifer your sister?*

[The candle lit up. Is there a back story there?]

Stacey: *Yes.*

Susan: *So, your sister that is with you, is her name Jennifer? Tell me more about the trouble in the attic. Is it the attic of this building or the one next door?*

Store owner: [Referring to the attic] *That actually goes over this, too.*

Stacey: *Attic.*

Susan: *Attic. She said attic again.*

Store owner: *Did you live up there?*

Susan: *Is there a—*

Stacey: *I'm afraid.*

Susan: *You're afraid? Are you afraid of something in the attic? We're on the second level, right?*

Store owner: *Did you die—*

Stacey: [Interrupts] *No.*

Store owner: *Upstairs?*

Geoport: *Sounds like* [can't make it out].

Susan: *Candle came on, so I'd say that's an affirmative. Are you afraid to go back up to the attic because you died up there?*

Store owner: *Did you die in the fire?*

Stacey: *Threat.*

Susan: *So, something in the attic is threatening you?* [The candle goes off.] *So, if something is threatening you in the attic, you can tell Stacey.*

Stacey: *Storage.*

Susan: *I understand. Are we safe if we went over next door and looked?*

Store owner: *Is there a danger in the staircase?*

Susan: *You need to give them a little time to answer in between. So, is the staircase going to the third level?*

Store owner: *That one lady felt threatened in the stairwell.*

Susan: *Is there danger on the stairs leading to the attic? Is there a spirit over there you are afraid of? Is there a spirit over there we should be afraid of? Are you and your sister both scared of the attic? Are you still here? Who is here with us right now? If you talk, Stacey can hear you through headphones.* [The candle lights up.] *Thank you. Can you tell me your name? Are you the little boy we were speaking with earlier?*

Store owner: *What is your sister's name?*

[The loud beeping of the temperature change indicator on the spirit box continued to go off, and I (Stacey) decided to stop due to the heat on my face becoming intolerable at that time.]

[Session ends.]

That night's investigation proved to be extremely eventful for my team and me. We bore witness to many paranormal encounters and witnessed

Hall's Grocery. *Sapulpa Historical Society.*

firsthand just how much of Sapulpa's history still lingers inside the historic walls of the Vintage Market. Whether they are ghosts from the past or spirits that might linger in the personal belongings of those long passed that sit on the shelves, one thing is certain: spirits do reside here, and it doesn't appear as if they ever wish to leave.

21

Box Portrait Gallery

Located in the downtown area of Sapulpa at 120 East Dewey Avenue is the Box Portrait Gallery. It's a quaint historic building that features two large open display windows in the front featuring some of the photographic masterpieces taken by the local photographers who reside there. It is also home to a sweet little black cat who goes by the name of Bob. (Don't let the name Bob fool you. The name doesn't pertain to her gender; rather, it refers to the little stub on her bottom where a tail would normally be found.) Bob is an attention-seeking creature in constant need of love. However, she is not the only attention-seeking resident that lingers in this historic location. There are a few more attention-seeking individuals who can be found in the upstairs location, a location that takes on an entirely different feeling should you be brave enough to ascend the age-worn stairs. Once there, you are instantly taken into another space and time as you step back into some of Sapulpa's deep, dark past.

Box Studio isn't just a place of phenomenal photography, but it appears its ghosts are also pretty impressive. The area located above the main floor of the Box Portrait Gallery is not generally open to the public; however, we were allowed to join an employee, Brennyn Petrone, as he let us upstairs to the darkened corridors of the building. Petrone shared one of his own experiences from previous visits at this location. He stated that when he was upstairs one day, he bent over to pick something up off the floor when he felt something—or someone—touched him from behind. Quickly turning around, he was surprised to find no one there at all. Other employees

Above: Dewey Avenue, 1940s. *Sapulpa Historical Society.*

Left: Bob the cat. *Amy McCue.*

The second floor of Box Photography. *Tanya McCoy.*

Box Photography, upstairs. *Tanya McCoy.*

Box Photography guillotine. *Amy McCue.*

have reported seeing couples dressed in late-1800s period clothing walking through walls.

We were privileged to be able to investigate this amazing building with Brennyn, and it absolutely did not disappoint.

As we climbed the time-worn stairs, we could hear the eerie sound of the creaking boards giving way as we slowly ascended step by step. Darkness engulfed us as we held our flashlights in front of us to help guide our way into the narrowing walkways above. When we reached the top of the stairs, we entered a large open area. There were various open doorways lining the walls that led off into the different areas of the building. No doors graced the entryways, having been removed several years before, offering us a clear view of all the rooms that surrounded us. Each room contained various items. In the middle of the hallway that leads off toward the back of the building is a long metal pipe extending the entire width of the building. It caused us to take a high step over it to avoid tripping as we walked throughout the area. Each room contained its own set of interesting items. In one room, an antique mirrored vanity with a single empty chair sits against a light brown canvas backdrop adorned with white blossoming flowers, inviting you to sit and gaze at yourself as you take a step back in time and soak in the history of a long-forgotten time. In another room, you can find various items, including a makeshift jail cell door, bars included. You will also find a re-created guillotine; it doesn't work, of course, but it's still very interesting to see. From various fireplace mantels to antique couches and other furniture, you can find all sorts of interesting items in this space.

After our initial walk-through, we decided to start our investigation. For our session, we decided to start in the front room, which housed only a dresser and a few chairs. There, we were able to gather some of the evidence that we believed was paranormal. We found that the spirits were not only talkative, but they were also helpful when telling us, "Watch where you go," as we headed back into the darker parts of the building. The first room we investigated is at the front of the building and overlooks the street. We began our session using the Geoport. Brennyn asked the spirits if they remembered the time one of them pocked him in the butt. The response we received was, "Yes, I do." Then the Geoport was noted to actually call him out by name. Shadow figures have been seen walking the halls in the upstairs area as well. As this location has a history as a bordello, it's no wonder the spirits continue to linger within these walls. It was a place known to host parties and pleasure, and it appears the party continues to go on. But don't feel sorry for the souls still lingering here. Petrone asked, "Are you stuck here?" The reply: "We kind of love you." Petrone does admit to saying hello and playing music when he goes to work upstairs. I (Tanya) think whatever he does seems to be for the benefit of the employees and the ghosts still hanging out. We believe this might be the reason the spirits seem to communicate well with him. Whatever the reason might be, one thing is sure: the spirits residing above the Box Portrait Gallery seem to be happy there, and it doesn't appear like they plan on leaving anytime soon.

22
Sapulpa Mercantile Exchange

Located next to Box Portrait Gallery is another quant little boutique for anyone wishing to visit the downtown area of Sapulpa. Small black and white tiles still line the entryway, along with large open glass window displays on either side. Once through the doors, you are greeted by friendly staff who are waiting to assist you in any way. This location was built in the early 1900s, but unfortunately, some of the building's history is still unknown.

The boutique has a large open floor plan extending along the entire length of the building. Clothing, shoes and handbags, along with other gifts, can been seen lining the walls and walkways. Directly ahead, a large open staircase leads you up to the second floor, where, in the past, other businesses once resided. Unfortunately for us, this area was off-limits at the time, since renovations were underway.

We spoke with one of the salesclerks on duty that night who was more than happy to share some of the ghostly tales associated with the location. It is believed that a few spirits continue to linger in this location. With this location just adjacent to Box, the belief is that the brothel actually extended between the buildings. Male and female spirits have been rumored to haunt this location, especially in the upstairs area. When asked, the salesclerk admitted to not being afraid of the spirits that continue to linger there. She states they have never caused her any harm, so she just continues with her day.

Do the spirits that still linger here possibly not even realize that they have passed away? Is it possible that they cannot see the living world around them? Perhaps they just wish to remain so they can hold on to a piece of their past in a place they once knew in the hopes of seeing it all once again. Those are the questions we often find we ask ourselves as we continue to search for the reasons spirits choose to linger here. Perhaps one day, we will be able to find a few of the answers.

23
TYLER FURNITURE

You can't mention the word *haunted* in Sapulpa without hearing the name Rick Tyler. Tyler was the owner and operator of Tyler Furniture, a store that has provided quality furniture to the Sapulpa area for over thirty-five years. Rick Tyler, a veteran of the U.S. Navy, serving from 1969 to 1975 under Dwight Eisenhower himself, represents a true example of what many of the residents of Sapulpa are like—hometown proud.

According to Mr. Tyler, one of the most haunted buildings in Oklahoma was his old building, located at 1517 East Hobson Avenue, along with various others extending to 2125 East Hobson Avenue. Tyler had owned this location since 1957, so he was well versed in the building's history. Over the years, this location has housed various businesses, such as a dance hall and a Golden Glove Boxing event center.

Jim Pace, the founder of Sooner Paranormal of Oklahoma (SPOOK), having researched over seven hundred cases, often frequented this location to conduct paranormal investigations. It was also a location he would take new investigators to for training due to its high concentration of paranormal activity. Unfortunately, these buildings were torn down, like so many other amazing historical buildings, due to the impact time and weather had on them. Still, many of their stories live on, as well as their ghostly inhabitants, passed down through the years in some of Sapulpa's most haunted history.

Tyler Furniture. *Sapulpa Historical Society.*

One such spirit is one known best as Walter Cake. His spirit was often witnessed lingering in the basement of the building. Walter would often appear as a red ball of light that would follow you around until you reached the top of the basement stairs. Once at the top, Walter would simply disappear. Other paranormal activity often reported at the locations were cameras being moved and investigators' being scratched and their hair pulled.

Another spirit that is believed to have haunted the location was one called the "cowboy." The cowboy is believed to have been an oil field worker who was killed. Video evidence obtained by Pace's team revealed a ghostly apparition of a man walking through walls.

Other ghostly activity reported included clocks that had not been working suddenly beginning to work again, as if fixed by a set of ghostly hands. They had not only been fixed, but they had been set to the correct time as well. Doors opened and closed on their own, and lights turned off and on by themselves when no one was present.

At one point, Tyler moved into the building to live. Paranormal activity appeared to take on a new life, as Tyler began to experience an increase in paranormal activity firsthand. One night, while he was in bed, he felt as if someone had sat down on the bed next to him. He also claimed that whenever he had his fan on, he could hear what sounded like three

Hobson Avenue. *Sapulpa Historical Society.*

different voices carrying on a conversation. When Tyler mentioned this to Pace, Pace instructed him to leave a recorder running across the room to see if he could capture any voices. Not only did Tyler manage to capture voices, but Pace was also able to tell him the names that were said during the investigation. He could also tell that the spirits were discussing Tyler himself. Candlesticks flew across the room at times, and teapot lids that had once been in the kitchen suddenly appeared in the bathroom. Tyler's cats were even witnesses to the paranormal activity. One particular closet seemed to vex them the most. The cats would often scratch at the door, but they refused to ever enter the closet.

At one point, Pace brought in another group from Oklahoma City to show them the activity he was experiencing. The group were all sitting on a couch when they heard some loud booms, and the couch, which they were all sitting on, moved across the room. At that point, the paranormal group loaded up their belongings and returned to Oklahoma City. When asked how he managed to live in such a haunted environment, Tyler said he never felt any threat from them.

Top: Post office interior, East Hobson Avenue, 1910s. *Sapulpa Historical Society.*

Bottom: East Hobson Avenue, from North Main Street looking east, 1910s. *Sapulpa Historical Society.*

The building has been gone for some time now, but one can only imagine what life must have been like living among so many spirits. But it leaves us wondering if these spirits remain in the area that once housed these buildings or if they moved on in search of a new home. Hopefully, wherever they may be, they will find happiness and peace in their afterlife.

24
THE BEARDED LADY

Located just a few blocks away from the museum is a small beauty shop known as the Bearded Lady. When we first arrived at the shop, I (Tanya) thought the location appeared small, but once we entered, I found it to be anything but small. Like many buildings constructed during Oklahoma's early years of statehood, this building has a small façade but extends much farther back, making it seem much larger inside. The first room you enter houses various barber chairs and even an antique one propped up in the back corner to remind us of the chairs that used to greet guests so many years ago. We were greeted by the owners, a very pleasant couple who welcomed us to their location. They began to share their own experiences that they'd had during their time at this location. They reported that items seemed to move on their own, and they said there was an incident in which a small boy who had been visiting one day was seen holding a conversation with someone sitting in the old antique chair, someone only he could see. After a quick visit and walk through the building, we set up our equipment and turned down the lights to begin our investigation there.

Intelligent responses were soon obtained from our series of questions, and once again, the equipment began to respond in various spots around the building. Words began to form a storyline, piecing together some of the history that appeared to be associated with this location. An image of a man slumped down against the wall, the veil of death clouding his eyes, started to form in my mind. Bloodstains soaked his shirt as a bullet wound began to emerge in the vision lying before me. I asked the owner if she was aware of any shootouts that might have occurred during the Prohibition days, since many of our responses were related to bootlegging and the law. She stated she was not aware of the buildings' entire history, but she did tell us of a bullet hole in the glass by the front door. Images continued to form in my mind, like a movie I was watching only when I was sitting in the middle of the scene.

Once we concluded our investigation, we returned to the museum to finish gathering up our things and meet the rest of the team. The images I had just witnessed weighed heavily on my mind, so once again, I turned to Rachel for possible answers. I asked her if she knew any history about the location or of a possible shootout between the law and bootleggers that occurred nearby. She shared with me the story of a local lawman who was not only involved in a shootout with bootleggers but was also guilty of being one himself. He was charged and found guilty but was only suspended for a few days before returning to work without further punishment for his own crimes. Once I returned home, I continued to research more about that location, hoping to find something more to add proof to what I had experienced that night. It was a few weeks later that I discovered what I had been searching for all along. An article told the story of a group of local lawmen who had engaged in a gunfight with bootleggers in front of a small shop next to an empty lot just a block away from the corner of Main Street, historic Route 66. For these spirits, it appears they continue in death as they did in life—only now they will live on forever as the spirits of Route 66.

25

CREEK COUNTY CHOPPERS

Creek County Choppers is not just a wonderful place to get a haircut or color, but for a paranormal investigator, it is also a place of intrigue and mystery. At 23 South Park Street in Sapulpa, owner Teresa Bailey has a beautiful facility full of pleasant employees who are always ready to help at the moment's notice. I (Stacey) found this out personally when I needed "viking hair" for a medieval festival. Within two days, I was in the salon chair. I also happened to win "best hair" in the festival contest. It was at this hair appointment that I discovered the employees have encountered resident ghosts who enjoy hanging out.

When you first enter the building, you might find yourself surprised at the magnitude and size of the shop. From an exterior view, one is led to believe the space is much smaller, but you will soon find just how misleading its outward appearance can be. As you enter, you are greeted with a high vaulted ceiling, every inch adorned with historic metal tiles, popular in decades past. Beautiful wood floors guide you deeper into the shop, which still contains much of the historic beauty from its early years. An ornate fireplace lines one wall, with classic chairs placed ideally beside it, offering guests a quaint and relaxing place to rest as they await their services. Just past the fireplace is a smaller room filled with toys and entertainment for younger guests should a client need to bring their child along for the day. Toward the center, various tables and alcoves present visitors with a chance to browse and shop for goods from local merchants and craftsmen around the area. Mirrors and chairs line the wall where clients sit to receive their

Residents of Sapulpa. *Sapulpa Historical Society.*

diverse services and treatments. As you travel farther in, you walk through another archway leading back to the restroom area and back office space, beyond the guest service area. When night falls, this area seems much more menacing than it appears in the light of the day. One might even feel the chill of its foreboding ambience should they be brave enough to venture into the unknown. Others might even consider one crazy to do so. Fortunately for us, we are that special level of crazy, and we soon found ourselves doing just that.

After we were given access to the building, we conducted an investigation and had quite a few verifications of the activity that occurred there. Immediately upon entering, Tanya McCoy felt a feminine presence. After finding all of the areas with electromagnetic frequencies (EMF) that could cause false readings, we began our investigation in the main salon area. We put out a thirty-six-foot-long tripwire to detect EMF from the children's playroom into the main entrance and up into the employee lounge. Cat balls that light up when they're moved were placed on each employee's station and in back rooms. Almost immediately, one of the cat balls began lighting up. Then another lit up on a different station, so much so that I considered changing the ball out for another—until it returned to normal. At one point, even the thirty-six-foot-long tripwire began going off in the children's playroom.

As I walked around, trying to sense the tingles I sometimes get—like the hair on the back of your head rising—I decided to wander into the area's closets and rooms. At that moment, I got one of the biggest scares I have ever encountered that was not paranormal. A life-size Halloween decoration in the shape of the distorted half bat/half man played by Gary Oldman in Bram Stroker's *Dracula* was being kept in the closet. From time to time, its location is changed to scare the wits out of employees. I did not receive that memo, and the owner, Teresa Bailey, got me, too. After taking a moment to ourselves and laugh off the scare, we moved to the break room to do an EVP (electronic voice phenomenon) session. Tanya often uses a ghost hunting app available on her phone. While I don't necessarily put faith in any device with built-in words, I do have to give her and the device credit, as I have been stunned at the results. The app spits out words related to what we are doing in real life or people connected to the locations we investigate. The first word we got that night was the name Christopher. We got another name that begins with A, and we were unable to identify if it was Adams, Andrew or Anderson. Other words that were mentioned were Oliver, Gavin and Brooklyn. When we asked if he was from Brooklyn, we got a positive affirmation when the spirit candle was lit up. Through additional questions, we learned the spirit had additional friends in the building. Other pieces of evidence gathered using the Geoport were the following statements: "you were," a slam followed by "why are you stopping," "take it off, boy," "be careful" and "look again." Overall, it was an enjoyable investigation with nothing that felt dark or heavy at any point. So, if you need a great cut or color and want to hear some fabulous ghost stories, be sure to check out Creek County Choppers.

26

CROSSROADS COOKERY

Several locations drew my (Tanya) interest around the town of Sapulpa. One such place is Crossroads Cookery. Located in one of the beautiful historic brick buildings that line Dewey Street, this restaurant offers an array of food choices, not to mention an amazing ice cream counter for those with a sweet tooth—like me. My team and I, along with Stacey and her team, were set to meet up that evening for a series of investigations in multiple locations around town. A few of us had decided to meet for dinner, and Stacey suggested Crossroads. As we entered the building, it became obvious that this place had more to offer than just a delicious sorbet. We were seated at a table just north of a long bar area, where servers moved around, tending to their guests. I sat quietly, attempting to focus on the energy I was feeling within the dark walls. On a whim, I decided to walk over to the bar area to order a drink. A sudden image popped into my head, and I found myself blurting out to the bartender, "So, who's the old cowboy spirit that wanders around up by the front door?" I caught a quick expression on his face as he responded, "We're not sure, but we often hear the sound of someone walking around there as well as on the stairs." I asked him if he knew what kind of activity occurred in or around the kitchen area, where a prankster spirit had been reported moving things or tossing them around. He said that he had been there only a few months and was seldom in the kitchen area, but he said he would ask around for me. He did say that the upstairs area always had a particular feeling to it and confessed that there were several artifacts from

The Cookery. *Sapulpa Historical Society.*

various regions stored there. My group continued with our talk as we ate our dinner, preparing for the night ahead. As we left the restaurant with our bellies full and our minds spinning, I made a mental note to return to Crossroads one day and, if we have time, perhaps reach out to the spirits that linger there. Hopefully, we will be able to discover their histories and perhaps the reasons they continue to live within the walls of Crossroads.

In December 2024, Stacey had the pleasure of returning to Crossroads Cookery to attend a Christmas party that was being held by the law firms she worked at. She shared a few experiences that a few of the guest reported experiencing that night. The following are her stories.

For the 2024 Christmas party for Creek County Law, a theme was chosen. The theme was 1920s speakeasy, and the party was held upstairs at Crossroads Cookery. An attorney and his wife were sitting on one of the couches with a container of poker chips sitting on the coffee table in front of them. The chips were going to be used as drink tickets for the employees and guests attending the party. As the two sat there, waiting for other employees to arrive, a poker chip popped up out of the holder and began circling in a figure-eight pattern on the floor and then came to a rest. No one had been near the poker chip holder or even the table at the time.

African art. *Tanya McCoy.*

The attorney looked at his wife and asked, "Did you see that?" His wife replied, "Yep." They were both left to ponder the paranormal activity they had just witnessed. With this building having such a long history steeped in illegal bootlegging, gambling and a bordello, I guess the spirits felt quite at home taking a chip of their own! However, I'm not convinced that it's only the local spirits that might be haunting this location—especially in the upstairs area. The upstairs area has recently taken on a new life of its own. Lining the walls of this vast location are multiple glass cases containing a multitude of African artifacts collected by the current owners of the building through their years of traveling. Various statues and pieces of tribal art are on display, as are multiple pieces of antique future and décor. With so many items that were created by the skilled hands of craftsmen and women, the likelihood that there's energy attached to these objects is pretty high. We often see this when we come across haunted inanimate objects, especially in museums. With so many layers of history and culture stored in one location, it's no wonder paranormal activity still resides in the Crossroads Cookery to this day.

27
The Patriot Café

Located along historic Route 66 is a quaint little café known as the Patriot Café. It's a small hometown café, a local favorite, offering some home-style delicious food for a very reasonable price—not often found in today's economy. Booths line the walls and tables and chairs crowd around the open space of the restaurant. As you enter the restaurant, you are greeted by the friendly staff behind the old countertop, which contains the register area and pitchers of fresh-made tea. An open window allows you to look back into the kitchen area, where food is prepared and passed through for the staff to receive. It's in this area that some of the paranormal activity was first witnessed. One day, while the staff was going about their daily routine, a fresh pitcher of tea was placed in the middle of the counter. As the server turned to leave, the tea pitcher went flying off the counter, hitting her. "You saw that, right?" she said, as the other employee verified that she had witnessed it as well. The pitcher had been sitting in the middle of the counter when it was tossed by a set of unseen hands toward the waitstaff.

There have been other ways that this mysterious presence has made itself known. Believed to be the spirit of a male entity, the tall, dark shadow of a man in a cowboy hat has been seen walking around the restaurant from time to time. Flashing lights appear as orbs in various areas around the building. One employee stated that there is a certain area toward the back of the building that she does not like to go into. She stated that whenever she has to go back there, she feels like she's being watched and never feels quite alone. Another employee stated that one night while closing up, they were cleaning the front lobby area when they heard a large crash coming from the kitchen area. They ran back to see what had happened and discovered that a large stack of dishes had come crashing to the ground.

It is believed that the spirit that lingers there actually followed the current owner when he moved locations from his previous business in Bristow, another small town located nearby. The staff have even given the cowboy a name; known only as Bill, this cowboy likes to make himself known to those who work there. He can even be heard whistling from time to time. Without personally investigating this location, we can't be sure if there are any other spirits haunting the Patriot Café, but I (Tanya) can attest to the fact that the food is worth stopping in for should you happen to be there. You may catch a glimpse of the infamous Cowboy Bill, but try not to freak out. If I were you, I'd steer free of the counter to avoid any flying tea pitchers!

CONCLUSION

Sapulpa, like so many other small, historic towns around the United States, offers travelers a peek into its historic past while giving a small-town welcome to all who drive along its streets. It's a chance to step away from the busy life of the city and visit some amazing small-town businesses and eateries along the way. If it's a quiet Sunday afternoon drive you seek or an encounter with some ghostly apparitions that linger along the dark and cloudy highways of the historic Route 66, then might we suggest a fun-filled trip to the sleepy town of Sapulpa, Oklahoma? You never know what you might find when you choose to travel the back roads of Oklahoma!

APPENDIX
TOOLS OF THE TRADE

We are often asked how we can know for certain a place is haunted or even if ghosts exist. The answer is quite simple: we cannot. We can have our beliefs, our feelings and even our senses to help us conclude in our own minds whether a place is truly haunted, but even with all of the new technical equipment that has been made to help us gather evidence of paranormal activity, it is all just based on theory in the end.

I (Tanya) have seen spirits since I was six years old. Many of my sightings were also witnessed by someone else at the same time. Does that prove ghosts exist? To me, it does, but to others who have not seen the same things, it does not. At the end of the day, everyone has their own beliefs. What you choose to believe is up to you. Since the night I witnessed my first spirit, I have been drawn to investigating the paranormal with the need to find answers. When the chance arose to join a paranormal team, I was thrilled. I spent years reading and researching some methods used by some of the well-known names in the paranormal field of research. I spent a few years with the team and then decided to branch out with a team of my own, the Oklahoma Paranormal Association (OPA).

The rise in new teams and lack of education on how to properly investigate were causing many haunted locations to refuse access to paranormal researchers. We hoped a formal class would help decrease the number of people breaking and entering and trespassing, and we also hoped to teach others to respect the spirits we visit. We have already seen remarkable success, and our class also provides the chance for people who would not normally investigate a haunted location to join us and learn how to investigate with the same equipment we use.

The equipment we use can be very costly, but those first starting out do not need to invest vast amounts of money into equipment. A simple compass is a tool that can detect a magnetic field disturbance. Dowsing rods can be used to ask questions or even locate an energy force. A pendulum (a crystal or metal point suspended from a string or chain) can help answer questions as well. All of these can be purchased for less than fifteen dollars. A digital camera and audio recorder can be a paranormal researcher's best friend. I remember the excitement I felt when I caught my first electronic voice phenomenon (EVP) and my first picture of a spirit. Many people have these pieces of equipment in their homes, and those who want to invest in their research may do so by recording straight to terabyte-sized DVR drives with night-vision or infrared cameras.

With the increase of interest in the paranormal, new equipment is being invented all the time to help researchers collect evidence, such as K2 meters, temperature guns, FLIR guns, parascopes and mel meters/gauss meters. These can become very costly.

For those not wishing to spend so much money, there is an alternative app available on smartphones, which already have built-in EMF detectors. Designed by Swedish app publisher Exelerus AB, Ghost Radio can be downloaded to a phone for a fraction of the cost of other equipment. I had never put much faith in phone apps used in paranormal investigating before, but I must say, this app has actually given us the same information the more expensive piece of equipment has, saying things that an app simply would not know on its own. Those who have downloaded it are usually quite happy with the results, and the app's inventors are polite and eager to work with others in developing further apps.

Investigators may spend thousands of dollars on equipment, but the best tools are one's own senses. The environment is the best indicator of any possible paranormal activity. Investigators should always be aware of their surroundings and note that any changes may be mundane as well as supernatural.

THE PARASCOPE

Created by Jeremy Jones, the proprietor of Paranologies, the parascope is a triboelectric meter made of a small square base with several transparent plastic rods standing straight up that light up in rainbow colors. The parascope detects different voltages of electricity in the surrounding air. We all have static electricity in our bodies, and Jones designed the meter in the hopes that the electricity we carry with us when we pass on can be detected by it. Unlike the K2 or other mel meters, which notice man-made energy as well as ghostly energy, the parascope is designed to detect free-floating static electricity and display its path of travel by lighting up the transparent plastic sticks or light source on top. In our investigations, we place parascopes in the areas where we tend to see a lot of shadowy figures or movement. I (Tanya) have found them to be very effective, and they are quickly becoming one of my favorite pieces of equipment.

EMF DETECTORS

There are several diverse types of EMF (electromagnetic field) detectors. The best known and widely used is the K2, a brand name made popular though exposure on many paranormal television shows. According to many paranormal researchers, spirits produce a magnetic field of energy. It is widely believed that spirits can control magnetic fields at will and can manipulate the equipment to light up when present. The K2 consists of an LED light-up scale. Unlike other EMF meters that can measure static EMF fields, the K2 can measure only magnetic fields. When the K2 comes into contact with magnetic energy, it transduces it into electrical energy, which becomes amplified, in turn lighting up one or more of the LED lights with their intensity depending on the energy levels. This helps the researcher to obtain answers from the spirit world by asking a spirit to answer questions by lighting up the LED lights. For example, if an investigator asks the spirit to please light up the meter if it is a female but the K2 fails to light up, that may be a "no" answer. If the investigator then asks the spirit to light the meter if it is a male and it does, then the investigator can draw the conclusion that the spirit is male. A K2 is a great tool to use when researching the paranormal, but an investigator must also be aware of receiving a false-positive reading. The K2 measures magnetic fields and is not programmed to receive them from only the spirit world. There are several other sources that can give a false positive, such as a cellphone. Receiving text messages, emails and other online updates can cause the K2 to light up. The best practice for an investigator is to put all smartphones on "airplane mode" and be aware that they may still produce false-positive readings. Other sources known to give off false-positive readings include copper wiring, CB radios, emergency vehicles, lights and walkie-talkies. It is best to be aware of your surroundings and to do a base reading of your locations.

THE FLIR

The FLIR is a name brand for an infrared camera used to detect heat signatures or forms of energy. It then converts this energy into an electronic signal, which is then converted into a thermal image. There are a number of different settings investigators can use, but the two most popular are the rainbow scale and the gray scale. The rainbow scale shows the difference in temperature from hot to cold, but we often prefer the gray scale, which works well for capturing shadow figures. The FLIR can be a good piece of equipment to own, but it can be very expensive for someone just starting out.

TEMPERATURE GUN

Another piece of widely used equipment is the temperature gun. This piece of equipment can run anywhere from forty to sixty dollars and can be found at local home improvement stores. The temperature gun is used to help detect any temperature changes in the air. It is believed that, for a spirit to manifest, it must first collect energy to gain strength to interact. Many believe spirits can take energy straight from the atmosphere, causing a noticeable drop in the temperature that is often described in ghost stories. Investigators should be aware of any windows, doors, fans or A/C units, which can all affect the temperature of the room.

EACH YEAR, IT SEEMS new devices are being created and experimented with in this field of study. Since the last description of devices that I (Tanya) first wrote in my 2015 book *Haunted Guthrie, Oklahoma*, several more pieces have been invented, tried and deemed successful. The following is a list of the updated equipment, vocabulary terms and methods, as well as a few that were previously used but not mentioned before.

The Candle (Available on Ghoststop.com)

The Spirit Candle "utilizes state-of-the-art magnetometer technology to detect EMF changes," according to the website Ghoststop.com. As energy levels increase, the spirit candle reacts by turning itself on and off, providing a visual aid to investigators that the ghosts have made themselves known! It has gained a tremendous popularity, given its price at under $100 and the fact that the candle is an item that will be familiar to spirits of all periods.

GS2 Laser Grid System (Available on Ghoststop.com)

This isn't just any ordinary laser grid system. It doesn't just map a room out a space and provide a visual for investigators; it also detects the temperature, direction and motion of shadows. It can even be used as an aid for 3D modeling. With light displays and sound, it can be used at a distance and works well for group investigations. You will always be able to provide solid evidence with this device.

SB7/SB7 Pro (Available on Ghoststop.com)

An absolute necessity for anyone who wants to hear the dead speak! For those into ITC (instrumental trans-communication), a ghost box, or spirit radio, as they are often referred to, is a must. With speed sweeps that take mere milliseconds, this ghost box picks up words and even sentences—unprecedented with other methods of communication with spirits. When paired with a Bluetooth speaker or even your phone, you can record and play back hours of communication and find the answers we all seek. This is one tool that you will always find in my backpack!

APF-D Processor

This is a tool that must be paired with an SB7 or similar device. Not only does it have a visual display to see when spirits speak, but it also has a recorder that allows you to immediately play sounds back on its unique loop feature. It also has adjustable speeds to allow you to have better control when listening to responses to your questions when conducting a spirit box session. According to ghoststop.com, it is compatible with SBox, SB7, SB11 and some other spirit boxes with a designated output for sweeping audio.

Tracer 2 Livewire

Imagine being able to see where a spirit is walking. Well, now you can! Simply lay the wire out straight and watch this device change from white to red to indicate where the spirits "walk." Don't forget to research where old doors may have been if you are dealing with remodels. Sometimes, the ghosts don't get the memo that a door is no longer there.

REM Pods

Using a very tiny telescopic antennae, REM pods emit their own EM field around the device so that when a paranormal entity comes into contact with it, it uses the lights and sounds to make its user aware of the presence of a form of energy. With its own sounds and lights, it's a great tool for investigators and can be heard from a great distance.

Toy Car from Amazon

This tool simply uses motion to go forward or backward, perfect for child ghosts to play with should you encounter one.

Parabolic Microphone (Available at Walmart)

This microphone allows you to enhance whispers and voices you cannot make out while investigating. Simply put in the earphones and point in the direction you hear a noise. Then pull the trigger and listen.

Flashlight

Not only can this tool prevent you from being the one thing that goes bump in the night, but it can also be a device used to answer yes and no questions. We use the Maglite brand that has the screw-on end. The mini light is best.

You will have to find the sensitive area that is the border between turning the light on and off. Once you can tap on the flashlight and see it briefly light up, you have discovered that border spot. You can then ask questions, and spirits will be able to communicate using the light.

Cat Balls

They are literally just that—cat toys. We suggest getting the ones that light up in the dark. They will light up in the dark when touched and can be seen across a dark room.

Laser Grid

You can purchase laser grid pens, and they will allow you to see shadow figures as you watch the light grids on a wall disappear. Place one on a mini tripod and point near any spot where shadow figures are seen.

DOWSING RODS

These L-shaped brass and copper rods have been used to find water for hundreds of years and have gained quite a following in the paranormal field. They're used to answer yes/no questions when they're crossed or uncrossed, and using them, one can uncover names, years and much more.

GEOPORT

One needs to only watch an episode of *Paranormal Lockdown* or *Portals to Hell* to see a Geoport in action. These amazing ITC devices allow you to literally hear the voices of the dead. Unlike any spirit box out there, this amazing device, created by George Brown Labs, uses EMF, vibrational waves and radio frequencies that even the inventor admits to not being able to understand. It uses a hacked radio plugged into an audio jack that Brown puts into these custom radio cases. Somehow, through the inventor's magic, the voices are incredibly clear, as there is less radio bleed in the background. It is the one device that completely eliminates the *ch ch ch* noise of a typical spirit box. Be prepared to wait on this device. There is a backlog, and at $2,000, it is one of the more expensive items out there. Each box is truly a piece of art and one of a kind. When you get serious, this is the one item you won't want to leave home without.

BIBLIOGRAPHY

The GhostHunter Store®. https://www.theghosthunterstore.com.

GhostStop. https://www.ghoststop.com.

"History of Sapulpa: Our Town, Our People, Our Sapulpa." Sapulpa Historical Museum. https://www.sapulpahistory.org/history-of-sapulpa.html.

"Local Author Pens Book About Bootlegger Cleo Epps." *Sapulpa Times*, July 16, 2019. https://sapulpatimes.com/local-author-pens-book-about-bootlegger-cleo-epps/.

Oklahoma Historical Society. https://www.okhistory.org.

"Sapulpa Somebodies That You've Never Heard Of. Probably: Richard C. Nelson." Sapulpa Historical Museum. November 28, 2021. https://www.sapulpahistory.org/sapulpa-somebodies/richard-c-nelson-c-1885-november-28-1921.

"A Traveler's Introduction to Oklahoma Route 66." Oklahoma Route 66 Association. https://oklahomaroute66.com/ok66history.

Whitney, Rachel. "This Week in Sapulpa History: 100 Years Ago, Nights of Terror." Sapulpa Historical Museum. January 1, 2023. https://www.sapulpahistory.org/did-you-know/100-years-ago-nights-of-terror.

———. "This Week in Sapulpa History: Sapulpa's Funeral Homes History." Sapulpa Historical Museum. April 21, 2024. https://sapulpatimes.com/this-week-in-sapulpa-history-sapulpas-funeral-homes-history/.

———. "This Week in Sapulpa History: Strange Time for Sheriff Strange." Sapulpa Historical Museum. July 3, 2023. https://sapulpatimes.com/this-week-in-sapulpa-history-strange-time-for-sheriff-strange.

Whitney, Rachel, and Kim Shockley. "This Week in Sapulpa History: Oklahoma's Only Woman Doctor: Dr. Elizabeth McCoy." Sapulpa Historical Museum. December 18, 2024. https://sapulpatimes.com/this-week-in-sapulpa-history-oklahomas-only-woman-doctor-dr-elizabeth-mccoy/.

Young, John W. *Sapulpa* (OK) *Herald*, October 24, 1934. https://gateway.okhistory.org/ark:/67531/metadc1525354/.

About the Authors

Tanya McCoy has been interested in the paranormal since she saw her first full-body apparition in her own home at the young age of six. She started doing research on the paranormal around 2001 and joined a paranormal investigation team around 2008. She started her own paranormal investigation team, the Oklahoma Paranormal Association (OPA), in 2011. As the founder of OPA and president of Paranormal Times Entertainments LLC, she is always teaching others, providing private investigations for public and private institutions. She has been featured on *My Ghost Story*, *Paranormal 911* and *Haunted Hospitals*, which are features on the Syfy Channel and the Travel Channel; she has also appeared in many articles, podcasts and newscasts. She enjoys doing background acting jobs and has done background work on some major motion pictures. She has authored and coauthored multiple books, including *Haunted Guthrie*; *Haunted Canadian County*; *Haunted El Reno, Oklahoma*; *Haunted Shawnee, Oklahoma*; *Haunted Oklahoma City*; and *Oklahoma's Haunted Route 66*. She is also a published children's book author, with her latest publication being an adapted version of her *Haunted Oklahoma City* book, *Spooky America's Haunted Oklahoma City*. Her *Spooky America's Oklahoma's Haunted Route 66* will be released in May 2025.

Aside from investigating the paranormal, Tanya has been a pediatric nurse for the past twenty-eight years and works with special needs children. She is currently working on her bachelor's degree in history. She is continuing to add to her book series, which will focus on her two favorite topics, history and the paranormal. She is also currently writing a fiction mystery novel, several children's books, a metaphysical collection and a true crime book of historic significance.

Stacey Price has been a paranormal investigator since 2013. She traveled to Germany, France and England in 2023 and will be visiting Ireland and Scotland in 2025, all in pursuit of paranormal experiences. A retired U.S. Air Force member, she conducts investigations with the precision to put forth only the clearest of evidence to the public. She was a research assistant on the book *Oklahoma's Haunted Route 66*, and this is her first book as a coauthor. In her down time, she is a master falconer and has spent nineteen years rehabilitating birds of prey. She also loves spending time in the great outdoors. Price and her husband, Brent, live on acreage in Kellyville, Oklahoma, where they are passionate about raising wagyu cattle.